CROYDON AIRPORT

THE AUSTRALIAN CONNECTION

Flights and other links between Croydon Airport and Australia

DOUGLAS CLUETT

London Borough of Sutton Leisure Services

THANKS AND ACKNOWLEDGEMENTS

Many people, by recording the history of British-Australia flights, in words and pictures, over the last seventy years have contributed to this book, and I am indebted to them all; but for help over the last few months I would especially like to thank the following:

Tony Brett Young for suggesting the theme of the book, and for helping with Australian research and material. For further help in research, for supplying information or illustrations, for allowing me to use their material, or for making their own research available for this book, I am particularly grateful to the following (in alphabetical order): Mary Batchelor, Joanna Bogle, Tom Carmody, Don Conway, Ted Crawforth, Rafael de Swarte (CoverCraft), Mr. and Mrs. R. Ellis, Jack Fuller, Ron Halliday, Mrs. Millicent Hamilton-Bradbury, Roger Jackson, Mrs. Molly Jones, Bob Learmonth, Mrs. Julie Little, Carla McGrorty, Mike Marshall, Charles Melville, Bert Nash, Rex Nicholls, Mr. D.J. Sawyer, Mike Stroud, Ted Wixted (Queensland Museum), and Mrs. Lynette Young.
Also: Shirley Edwards for designing the book; George Jenkinson and Bert Crawshaw for photographic work; Sally Hunt and Peggy Barnett for typing virtually illegible manuscripts; June Broughton for advice, instant copy-editing and proofing; and Roy Smith, Director of Leisure Services, for deciding to publish. Thanks are also due to Elaine Jones and the staff of the Quadrant Picture Library for their help. Despite all this, the responsibility for mistakes of course remains mine.

Douglas Cluett

ILLUSTRATIONS ACKNOWLEDGEMENTS

Back cover: Photograph, Quadrant Picture Library;
Caricature, Charles Couper Dickson

1, 13, 23, 46–50, 52, 54–56, 58, 76: Mrs. Molly Jones
2, 4–8, 20, 21, 34–37, 39, 40, 44, 65, 70, 73, 82, 86, 87, 88, 90, 91, 102–104: Quadrant Picture Library
10: The late N.J.W. Clench (via Mr. K.J. Clench)
11, 22, 30, 42, 64, 67, 77, 79, 83, 95: The A.J. Jackson collection (Roger Jackson)
16: Tiger Club/Jeanne Frazer
17: British Aerospace/Mike Stroud
19, 26, 27: Queensland Newspapers Ltd.
25, 125: Croydon Airport Society
28: Rafael de Swarte/CoverCraft
31, 64: Science Museum (Major Richard's scrapbooks)
33: The late Mr. W.L. Hatcher
41: Mr. W.A. (Bill) Webb
43: Mrs. Julie Little/Croydon Airport Society
51: Photo donated by Mr. Kevin Brown
57: Wing Commander R.V. Fiddick, R.A.F. (Rtd.)
59–62: Mrs. H.J. Ellis
69, 72, 92: Post Office Archives
75: Jeff Meddle
80: The late Jack Crowson
81: Mr. A.B. Coates
84: Capt. R.U. Price
85: Photo: E.A. McLennan
89: Post Office (Crown Copyright)
93, 94: Mrs Audrey Sammons
98: Philip Jarrett
100, 101: Mr. D.J. Sawyer
106, 107: Ron Halliday
108, 109: Ewart Sanders
110, 111, 112, 114, 116, 117: Rex Nicholls
113, 115: Don Conway
118/119; The late Charles Sammons/Mrs. Audrey Sammons
120, 121, 123, 124: Croydon Advertiser

Copies of the above are now in the Heritage Division's Local Collection, Sutton Central Library, as are other illustrations used.

First published 1988

Central Library, St Nicholas Way,
Sutton, Surrey SM1 1EA Tel: 01-661 5050

ISBN 0 907335-17-9

Printed and bound in Great Britain by Drogher Press, Christchurch, Dorset

FOREWORD

I am delighted that the London Borough of Sutton's Leisure Services team have chosen the year of Australia's Bicentennial Celebrations to publish this book. Croydon Airport's flying links with Australia are indeed numerous — not just with intrepid explorers; names like Amy Johnson, Bert Hinkler, Charles Kingsford-Smith, but also with commercial links from the start of aviation — passenger, postal and freight services, and other connections as told here.

As a boy living in Eire in the 1930s, I can well remember my Uncle, Horace Drury, arriving by air at Dublin Airport from Croydon Airport. I recall that in those days, flying to Dublin was so unusual that the names of the passengers appeared in the Dublin paper.

It is remarkable that so many good quality and detailed photographs still exist, highlighting the many great aviation achievements between Britain and Australia, and I am sure readers in both countries will find this book fascinating and rewarding.

Peter Gadsden.

Sir Peter Gadsden, GBE, AC.
Chairman,
The British-Australia Bicentennial Committee

INTRODUCTION

The publication of this book is timed to coincide with an air show on the Croydon Airport site on 30th May 1988. Like the air show, it is intended to be a contribution towards the celebration of the Australian Bicentennial, together with those of other local authorities with historic links with Australia. Our major links are through Croydon Airport, which at one time was entirely within the present boundaries of the London Borough of Sutton, and, after an enlargement of the airport in 1928, eighty-six per cent so. Croydon, because of its role between 1920 and 1939 as London's major airport — and therefore Britain's major airport — was intimately concerned with the pioneering, record-making and record-breaking flights during those years, the years of the establishment of international and long-distance flight. Moreover, it was concerned with the setting-up first of experimental, and then regular, air mail and passenger services between Britain and the world beyond Europe.

This was particularly true of flights within the British Commonwealth, and the establishment of what were called the Empire Air routes. Imperial Airways was formed in 1924, and its home base from the beginning was Croydon. A major goal was the forging of a regular link with Australia, on the opposite side of the world. For the pioneering airmen and airwomen a flight between Britain and Australia, and the beating of others' records between the two, was the passport to fame and fortune for those who could achieve it and capture the headlines. At the same time they were trail-blazers for the regular scheduled flights to come. These are the stories told here; with other links too, between Croydon Airport and Australia.

Some people made their last take-off from England from Lympne (pronounced 'Lim'), a Croydon 'satellite' near Hythe on the Kent coast, thus saving a few precious miles of fuel. Croydon, however, featured in some way in almost every flight between the two hemispheres in the formative years. In the early days, the name linked on the other side of the world with Croydon was Darwin. All the early flights finished there, by the inlet of the Timor Sea known as Port Darwin, with its airport at Fannie Bay, at the north-western tip of Australia; geographically the most convenient point before or after crossing the Timor Sea, the first or last hazard in the long flight across the world. Later, other airports on the 'north west aerial frontier' were used for the first touch-down; but the two names Croydon and Darwin will be for ever honoured above all others in the story of British-Australia flight.

This book is not intended to be exhaustive, though most relevant flights, including some unsuccessful ones, are touched on. Its arrangement is largely chronological, except that relevant flights of major fliers are dealt with in one section. Like its predecessor, *The First, the Fastest and the Famous,* this book can to some extent be considered as an appendage to our 'History of Croydon Airport' series. With a few exceptions, the illustrations used here have not been used in our previous publications, and some have never before been published.

Douglas Cluett
Heritage Officer
March 1988

FIRST FLIGHTS

1

1. Lieutenants Raymond John Paul Parer (left) and John Cowie McIntosh being received at Government House, Darwin, by the Administrator of North Australia, the Hon. Staniforth Smith (the ghostly-looking victim of camera flare, caused by the reflective quality of his white suit) after their flight.

FIRST SINGLE-ENGINED FLIGHT TO AUSTRALIA — IN A CROYDON REBUILT AIRCRAFT

The second aeroplane to reach Australia from Britain under its own power was a single-engined de Havilland D.H.9 flown by Raymond Parer and John McIntosh. The first had been the Vickers Vimy, G-EAOU, with two engines and a crew of four, led by Ross Smith as pilot, and his brother Keith as navigator; winning an Australian Government prize of £10,000. This flight started from Hounslow, on November 12th 1919, and reached Darwin on December 10th after 135 hours in the air, spread over twenty-eight days. Hounslow, to the north of London, was London's first customs airport — but for only nine months, until March 1920, when that distinction was transferred to Croydon.

Roy Parer and John McIntosh were Australians who had served in the Royal Flying Corps and who decided to return home by air. Originally they had hoped to win the prize which Ross and Keith had won, the terms for which required the winner to be the first Australian airman to fly a British aircraft from the UK to Australia within thirty consecutive days. They also left from Hounslow — on January 8th 1920, in an aircraft which had been converted at Croydon from the World War I D.H.9 two-seater day-bomber to a civil aircraft by Mr. (later Sir) Frederick Handley Page's Aircraft Disposal Company, then occupying the large workshops of what had been National Aircraft Factory No.1. The flight, not without its problems and misadventures, took much longer than the Vimy's: by the time they reached Darwin the D.H.9 had its third radiator, third undercarriage, and fifth propeller; and 206 days had elapsed (it was the 2nd of August when they touched-down at Fannie Bay, Port Darwin).

John McIntosh died in a flying accident in 1921. Parer won the first Australian Aerial Derby, and later was a pioneer of aviation in New Guinea, before becoming a farmer near Brisbane, where he died. ●

2

2. The A.D.C. D.H.9 after a crash-landing: presumably that which occurred at Culcairn, between Sydney and Melbourne, on the last leg of the flight across Australia from Darwin. The aircraft was repaired and is now preserved in Australia. The large 'P.D.' on the fuselage reflects the financial support for the flight given by Peter Dawson's, distillers of Scotch whisky (a bottle of which they conveyed as far as Melbourne for presentation to the Prime Minister, Billy Hughes).

Alan COBHAM

Sir Alan Cobham, K.B.E., A.F.C.

3

COBHAM'S FLIGHT TO AUSTRALIA, 1926

One of the most famous aircraft of the 1920s, the de Havilland D.H.50 G-EBFO, was flown to Australia by one of Britain's greatest pioneer fliers, Alan Cobham. G-EBFO started life as an ordinary commercial aircraft, designed to carry three passengers. It served first with the de Havilland Aeroplane Hire Service, and then was loaned to Imperial Airways at Croydon in 1924. Alan Cobham had served in the R.F.C. and R.A.F. before entering civil aviation. He joined de Havilland Aircraft in 1921. By 1926 he already held a number of records, had won the King's Cup Air Race, and had made long-distance flights, notably in G-EBFO: flying Sir Sefton Brancker, Director of Civil Aviation, to India and Burma in 1924; and, with 'FO modified to a D.H.50J by the substitution of a more powerful engine, flying from Croydon to Cape Town and back between November 1925 and March 1926.

Cobham had long desired to make a flight to Australia. The Cape flight, he said later, at a reception after he had achieved the trip to the other side of the world and back, had been necessary before he could command support for 'the bigger enterprise' (the backer he found was Sir Charles — later Lord — Wakefield, the Castrol oil millionaire). The flight began in the ▶

4

4. *Sir Alan Cobham in a D.H.82A Tiger Moth at the National Air Day, Hanworth, 1932.*

5

5. *G-EBFO the famous D.H.50 (the second to be built) seen at Croydon before its original 230hp Siddeley Puma engine was replaced by a more powerful 385hp Armstrong Siddeley Jaguar air-cooled radial engine. This was to give it extra power for take-off from high altitude aerodromes on its Cape flight, but was also part of a re-build necessitated by a crash-landing at the de Havilland aerodrome at Stag Lane near Edgware.*

6. *G-EBFO in Imperial Airways' service at Croydon. In the cockpit is H.S. Broad, about to fly to Prague (a distance of 600 miles) with Lord Thomson, Secretary of State for Air (centre) and Sir Sefton Brancker (left), bound for the opening (by President Jan Masaryk) of the Third International Aero Exhibition in Prague. Posing for the cameraman with an even odder gesture than Sir Sefton (the original* Flight *caption said that they were 'in merry mood') is Mr. Frank Hodges, MP, Civil Lord of the Admiralty, who was bound for Vienna. In 1930, both Sir Sefton and Lord Thomson were to die in the R101 disaster. On this day, however, they left Croydon at 7.30am and arrived in Prague at 4.40pm. The date was May 30th, 1924.*

6

7

7. *With G-EBFO as a seaplane, Cobham approaches his perfect touch-down on the Thames, on October 1st, 1926 with crowds thronging the banks to welcome him home, after clocking-up 28,000 miles to Melbourne and back.*

early morning of June 30th 1926, from the Medway at Rochester. The D.H.50 had been fitted with seaplane floats by Short Bros. Ltd., as so much of the route to be travelled lay over water. Cobham took thirty-seven days to fly the 11,380 miles to Port Darwin. On the way occurred the tragic death of A.B. Elliott, the engineer who had accompanied him to the Cape and back. They were flying between Baghdad and Basra, when Elliott was hit by a bullet and wounded in the arm and lungs, injuries from which he died at Basra. The bullet was fired by a Bedouin hunter, apparently accidentally, when he was frightened by the aircraft roaring overhead. Cobham's engineer when he reached Darwin, on August 5th, was Sergeant Alan Ward, lent to him by the R.A.F. Here the aircraft's floats were changed back to wheels for the rest of the flight to Melbourne; the reverse procedure taking place when he left for Britain from Darwin on September 5th. The journey ended on the Thames on October 1st when Cobham executed a gentle touch-down opposite the Terrace of the House of Commons, where his wife and an official welcoming party including the Speaker of the House of Commons; Sir Samuel Hoare (Secretary of State for Air); and Sir Sefton Brancker, received him.

Cobham, by these long-distance flights, did much to survey and pioneer what later became the 'Empire air routes'. It is perhaps interesting that Wilson's Grammar School, then in Camberwell, where he was educated, should later (after his death — he died in 1973) be moved to where it is at present, on the old flying-field of Croydon Airport, very near to the site of the airport buildings that existed before 1928, which Cobham knew so well, and which were the scene of such triumphs as his return from the Cape in 1924. He was knighted in 1926 after the flight to Australia.

G-EBFO was sold to West Australian Airways Ltd., in 1929, and re-registered as VH-UMC. ●

8

8. *(Above) Stanley Melbourne Bruce (later Viscount Bruce of Melbourne) and his wife in front of a Handley Page H.P.32 Hamlet at the Imperial Conference air display at Croydon on October 23rd 1926. Not a very successful aircraft, this was the only one built. It had first flown two days before, and it flew last with its original engines four days later. It was re-engined twice but flew only two or three times more — once only, with its final engines — and was scrapped in 1929. The original caption for this picture in* Flight *said: 'Just the thing for Australia?' Perhaps not. Bruce was a coalition Prime Minister (Nationalist-Country) serving from 1923 to 1929. Born in Melbourne, but a graduate of Cambridge University, he was often regarded as more English than Australian. He represented Australia in Britain's war cabinet in World War II, and received his peerage in 1947. He died in 1967.*

TWO AUSTRALIAN PRIME MINISTERS AT CROYDON

When Imperial Conferences were held in the 1920s and 1930s, a usual feature was an air display at Croydon Airport, with the object of impressing what *The Aeroplane* called the Premiers, Potentates and Powers. Delegates were able to see not only the British and foreign aircraft normally using the airport, but representatives of the latest in civil and military aircraft brought in for the occasion. In 1930 *The Aeroplane* said, a little rudely: 'On the whole the various types were quite smartly groomed for the occasion, and all had little official placards with their names, engines, power, loading, weight, range, and other intimate details more or less innaccurately [sic] set forth by a higher authority than the maker's. The sign-writing was very neat and of standard pattern, which is after all the main thing (as the delegates would hardly remember or understand the figures).'

Here, on two different occasions, are two different Australian Prime Ministers at Imperial Conference air days at Croydon. ●

9. *(Below) From left to right: Mr. (later Sir) Frederick Handley Page; Mr. Charles Fairey (of Fairey Aviation and President of the Royal Aeronautical Society); Mr. James Scullin, Prime Minister of Australia; and Air Vice-Marshal C.L. Lambe, at Croydon Airport on October 25th, 1930. This was the Imperial Conference held in the shadow of the R101 disaster (which had happened on October 5th). James Henry Scullin was Prime Minister in the Australian Labor government of 1929–32. His period of office was an unfortunate one, coinciding with the Great Depression, and he lost power in a landslide after his party split. He died in 1953.*

9

10

10. IMPERIAL AIRWAYS AIRLINER NAMED AFTER AUSTRALIAN CITY

The Handley Page W10-1, G-EBMM, *City of Melbourne* was the first of a fleet of four W10s named after Commonwealth cities. The others were G-EBMR *City of Pretoria*; G-EBMS *City of London*; and G-EBMT *City of Ottawa*. All plied between Croydon and the continent, on behalf of Imperial Airways. The W8s, 9s, and 10s were the first purely civil Handley Page aircraft, following their 0/400 World War I bomber civil conversions and their variants. The W10 carried sixteen passengers. *City of Melbourne* flew for Imperial Airways from 1926 until 1933. (One of its W8 predecessors, G-EBBH, had been named originally, in 1922, *Melbourne* but this had been changed to *Prince George*.) In 1933 'MM was, with its surviving sister 'MR, sold to Sir Alan Cobham for his National Aviation Day Displays Ltd., renamed *Youth of New Zealand*, and used for joy-riding. It was converted to a tanker for the purpose of refuelling Cobham's Airspeed Courier in the air for his attempted non-stop flight to India in September 1934, but after refuelling Cobham over the Isle of Wight, and the removal of the tanks, a tailplane failure caused it to crash and burn out near Aston Clinton in Buckinghamshire whilst flying to Coventry to rejoin the Air Display on 22nd September. (Cobham's flight ended at Malta when an attempt at a second air refuelling, from G-EBMR, failed. This aircraft, last of the W10s, was then scrapped.) •

11

11. Bill stands by Red Rose.

THE SAGA OF BILL LANCASTER, CHUBBIE MILLER, *RED ROSE* AND *SOUTHERN CROSS MINOR*

The story of Captain William Newton Lancaster and Mrs. Jessie Maude 'Chubbie' Miller has all the elements of a sensational novel or film: high adventure, romance, sex, adultery, betrayal, violent death, a dramatic murder trial, death in the desert, and a mystery ended after twenty-nine years (it has in fact become a television film and video under the title *Victims of Passion*). And it all began, in a sense, at Croydon Airport. It was on 14th October, 1927, that Bill and Chubbie set out from there to fly to Australia and fell in love on the way.

Lancaster was an ex-R.A.F. pilot, twenty-nine years old. Although born in Birmingham, his family were a Croydon family who moved back south soon after his birth. Mrs. Miller was an Australian, married, not particularly happily, to an Australian journalist. She had come alone on a six-month trip to Britain. She was called 'Chubbie' as tall men are called 'Tiny', and short men are called 'Lofty'. She was, in fact, a compact brunette, only five feet one inch high, and weighing only seven stones. She was twenty-five years old. They met at a party in Baker Street. Lancaster was planning to make his name by being the first to fly solo to Australia. Chubbie abandoned thoughts of returning home by sea and determined to go with him. She offered to raise fifty per cent of the total cost of the flight through her Australian contacts; and the fact that she was a woman would help enormously with the publicity. He ▶

12

12. Bill and Chubbie together in the Avian at Croydon before departure.

13

13. Bill and Chubbie finally reached Darwin on March 19th, 1928. The landing field was flooded from torrential rain they had just flown through, and they landed in two inches of water. They were not expected, and the first official who approached them waved them away as they splashed towards him, saying they had to be checked by the health inspector first. However, this was made up for subsequently by the people of Darwin, and a civic reception was accorded them. Here they are being received by the Mayor of Darwin.

agreed. Even if not solo, it would still be the first flight to Australia in a light aircraft.

Bill's aeroplane was an Avro 594 Avian III, G-EBTU, *Red Rose*. The name, of course, relates to the royal house of Lancaster, but it also referred to Lancaster's mother, an eccentric woman who dressed like a nun, dabbled in the occult, and was involved with a fringe-religion/charity organisation (the 'Mission of Flowers') whose members gave themselves flower names. She was Sister Red Rose. The aircraft had a Cirrus II engine, built by the Aircraft Disposal Company at Croydon.

The couple were seen off from Croydon by the wife of the Australian High Commissioner, Lady Ryrie; and by Lancaster's parents, his wife Kiki, and his two daughters. Chubbie watched as Bill kissed Kiki goodbye (she got a kiss from Kiki herself), before they left on their 13,000 mile journey. They reached Australia, but it took five months; and Bert Hinkler, starting months later, also in an Avian, beat them to it. On the way they were delayed by one major accident, and several minor ones; Chubbie learned to fly; and they became lovers.

Neither returned home, but went to live together in America. In 1932, Chubbie briefly took a new lover in Bill's absence. After his return, the man, Haden Clarke, died of a gun-shot wound. Lancaster was accused of murder, but acquitted (suicide was possible). The pair, reunited, returned to England. Lancaster had to do something to make a living. He tried for a job with a small airline flying from Croydon, but failed. He felt then that something spectacular was needed to recoup his fortunes, and decided to try to beat Amy Johnson's record to Cape Town. His father bought him, for this purpose, another Avian, the 616 Avian V, G-ABLK, *Southern Cross Minor* which had belonged to Charles Kingsford-Smith, who had attempted a flight from Melbourne to England in it (unsuccessfully). *Red Rose* had been sold in Australia, becoming VH-UTO and ending its life, burnt out, in New South Wales in 1936.

Lancaster set out in *Southern Cross Minor* in April 1933, but disappeared over the Sahara. It was twenty-nine years later, in 1962, that the wreck was found with his partially-mummified body beside it. Also present was his log-book, in which he had kept an account of the last eight days of his life as he died of thirst.

Throughout the pages he addresses both his 'darling mother' and 'darling Chubbie', whom it is clear he had never stopped loving, and some of his concern is for them to 'make it up and meet' (his mother had never accepted the relationship). On the cover he wrote (addressing it to both of them): 'Please read this together for my sake. Bill — my last wish'. But of course, by the time it was found it was too late for that, though Chubbie, by then remarried for twenty-six years, survived to read it.

Bill Lancaster died, just one year later, within a few hours, than the man he had been accused of killing. Chubbie died in 1972. ●

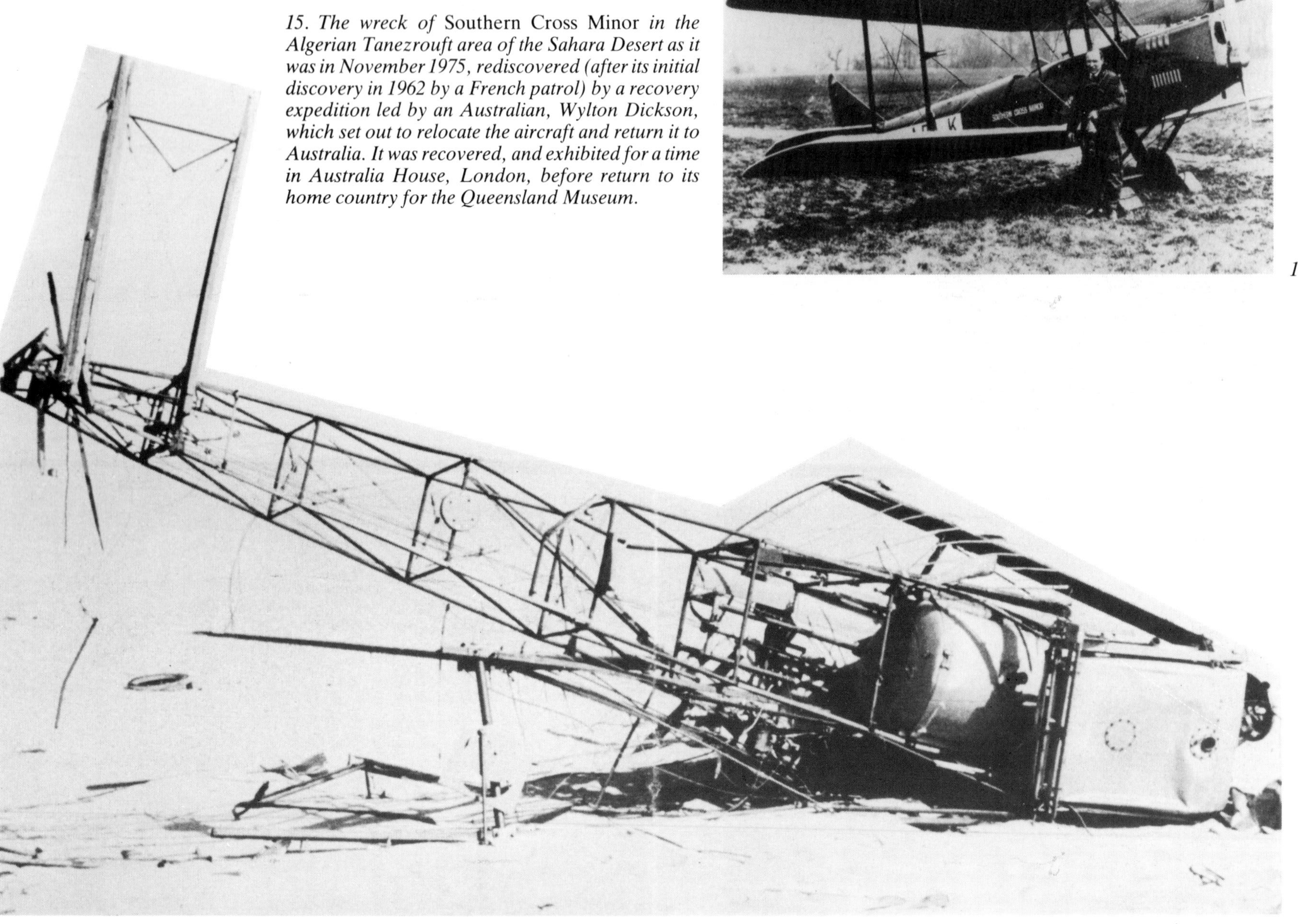

14. Bill Lancaster stands beside Southern Cross Minor, *G-ABLK (when flown by Kingsford-Smith it bore the Australian registration VH-UQG).*

15. The wreck of Southern Cross Minor *in the Algerian Tanezrouft area of the Sahara Desert as it was in November 1975, rediscovered (after its initial discovery in 1962 by a French patrol) by a recovery expedition led by an Australian, Wylton Dickson, which set out to relocate the aircraft and return it to Australia. It was recovered, and exhibited for a time in Australia House, London, before return to its home country for the Queensland Museum.*

16

16. *Bert Hinkler with the Avro 581E Avian prototype, G-EBOV, at Hamble (where it was built) in 1927. (Production Avians I, II, and III were designated Avro 594s.)*

BERT HINKLER: FIRST SOLO FLIGHT TO AUSTRALIA – FROM CROYDON – BY AN AUSTRALIAN, FEBRUARY 1928

Sixty years before Australia's Bicentennial year, an Australian became the first person to fly solo from Britain to Australia, and also the first person to reach Australia in a light aircraft.

Herbert John Louis Hinkler, one of the world's greatest pioneers of flight, was born at Bundaberg, Queensland, a town and district of some 13,000 people, on December 8th 1892. His father was John William Hinkler, of German birth, and his mother had been Frances Atkin Bonney. John Hinkler worked in the local sugar-cane industry. Bert had just turned eleven when the Wright brothers made their first 'flight' (of twelve seconds); but even before that he was fascinated by the idea of flying: studying ibises and gulls, and reading all he could on the theories of flight. At the age of twelve he was building model 'aircraft', and then an 'aviette' — a pair of wings with arm-sockets. At the age of nineteen he built a glider which rose thirty feet into the air.

In 1912, Hinkler met an early 'barnstormer' flier called 'Wizard' Stone — Bert was able to put him right on a question of wing-bracing — when Stone came to Bundaberg. Later, Hinkler toured New Zealand ▶

17

17. *Hinkler with the Sopwith Dove, a civil, two-seat, version of the well-known Sopwith Pup of World War I fame. Ten of these were built, and it was in this one that Hinkler had planned to fly to Australia and win the Australian government's £10,000 prize in 1919.*

18

18. Hinkler with the Avro 534 Baby, G-EACQ, in which he made his first attempt to fly to Australia, in 1920. Here, he is wheeling it out of its hangar at Croydon.

19

19. G-EACQ, restored, in the Queensland Museum.

with him, before making up his mind to go to England 'to see the flying with my own eyes and see what the prospects of the game are over there'. At the age of twenty-one he left Sydney, arriving in England at Easter 1914. He got a job with the Sopwith Aviation Co. at Kingston; but in August the war came, and Hinkler joined the Royal Naval Air Service, became a gunner, and flew on bombing raids on Germany in Handley Page 0/400s. In July 1918 he qualified as a pilot, and in the same month wrote to his parents about his post-war hopes: 'I shall be terribly disappointed if I do not have a machine to fly back to Bundy . . . '.

After the Great War he began to plan a flight to Australia in earnest. Originally he hoped to do it in a machine made by his old employers, Sopwith, and hoped they would sponsor him. Then came the announcement of the Australian Government's offered prize, and Sopwith wanted him to make the attempt on those terms. Hinkler's nomination for the attempt was the first received, but delays over an agreed route occurred, and Sopwith's sold the Dove earmarked for Hinkler's trip. Hinkler withdrew in disgust, and joined A.V. Roe and Company, makers of Avro aeroplanes.

Avro were developing a new aircraft, ▶

20. Hinkler adjusts the Croydon-built A.D.C. Cirrus I engine of his Avian. A.D.C. stood for Aircraft Disposal Company, the firm originally set up by Frederick Handley Page in the old National Aircraft Factory premises at Croydon to dispose of surplus World War I aircraft parts.

20

21

21. The Avian, with folded-back wings, at a Hampshire Air Pageant in 1927. Hinkler was an inventor, and this method of folding the wings (for transporting or housing the machine) was devised by him.

22

22. *Halfway there! Hinkler with G-EBOV at Karachi on the way out to Australia. He arrived on the 14th, and left on the 15th February 1928.*

the Avro 534 'Baby', which Hinkler tested. He hoped this aircraft would get him to Australia, but by the time its final tests were completed, Ross and Keith Smith had collected the prizes and a knighthood each. Bert, however, acquired the second prototype Baby, G-EACQ, and set out to attempt the first solo Australia flight. He left Croydon on May 31st, 1920 (a very cold morning). He got as far as Turin, setting a new record for a non-stop long-distance flight, but had to turn back there because the War Office warned against the necessary over-flights of Arab territory where armed conflicts were breaking out. Hinkler then shipped the Baby to Australia in 1921, setting up, whilst there, an Australian long-distance record of 800 miles non-stop, Sydney to Bundaberg, in nine hours. The Baby remained in Australia when Bert returned to England, becoming VH-UCQ. Restored, it is now in the Queensland Museum.

Back in England, Hinkler continued flying for Avro, and also entered contests and races, many of which he won, usually backed by his employers. In 1927, Hinkler reached his 35th birthday, and began again to think of a solo flight to Australia. There was a new Avro, the Avian, and Bert had already flown G-EBOV, the prototype with an 80hp A.D.C. Cirrus I engine (again — Croydon built) non-stop to Latvia, 1,200 miles, in ten and three quarter hours on 27th August. He sought financial backing, but 1927 had been a year of fatal accidents in long-distance flying, and he met with no success. He decided, therefore, to go it alone. His departure was planned from Croydon on Tuesday 7th February, 1928. On the day before, he was at the airport, worrying about his wife's non-arrival from Southampton to see him off. (She would have liked to accompany him on the flight, but he had filled the passenger cockpit with a reserve fuel tank.) Nancy's car had broken down on the way, and she had to take a slow train. It would be after midnight when she reached London. He went to meet her, and it was two o'clock a.m. when they reached the Aerodrome Hotel to spend the night. He had to be up again at four-thirty on a cold, damp, misty morning: but he was determined to go ahead.

Bert left at 6.50, with a *Times* atlas to navigate by, some samples (probably commercial) of cigarettes and Scotch whisky (cf Parer and McIntosh) and a letter from the Australian High Commissioner to the Australian Prime Minister saying: 'I am handing this letter to Mr Hinkler, the airman, in the confident hope that he will be able to carry it ►

23. *Bert Hinkler immediately after landing at Fannie Bay, Port Darwin. Dr. Cecil Cook, Quarantine Officer, was the first to welcome him. The date was 22nd February 1928 and Hinkler had just made a ten and a half hour flight over the dangerous Timor Sea.*

23

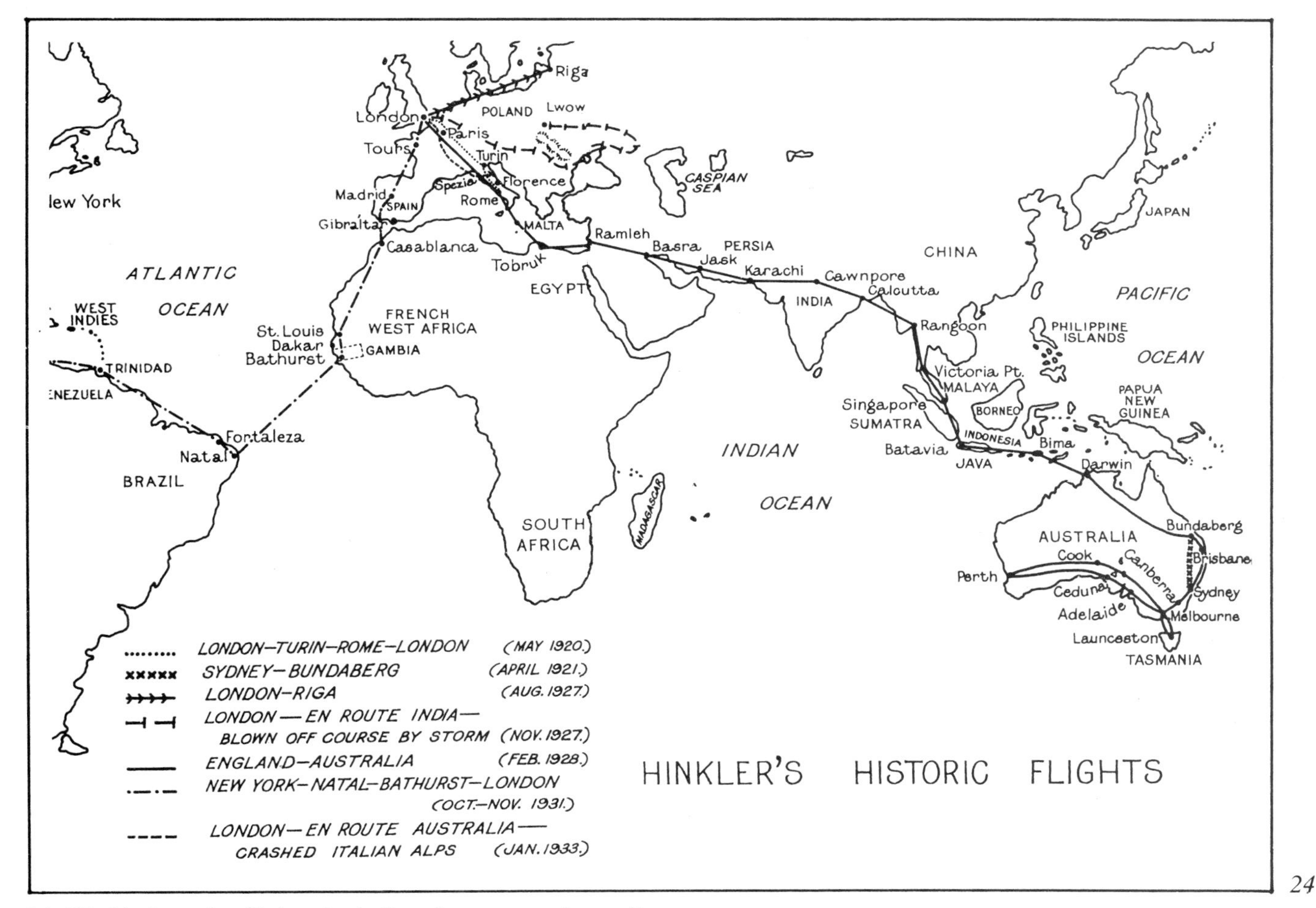

24

24. Hinkler's major flights; including the route to Australia.

by aeroplane from this country . . . '. The first leg of the flight was non-stop to Rome in twelve and three-quarter hours, a new record. By the time he was halfway the newspapers were taking notice: London to India in seven days was another record. It was at Singapore, to which Miller and Lancaster had returned weeks before with their damaged *Red Rose* after crashing it at Muntok, that Hinkler caught up with them. Some sympathisers of Bill and Chubbie there had declared that Hinkler would not be allowed to go further because he had not given them time to repair their aircraft and complete the flight. However, Bill recognised that Bert had allowed a reasonable time to elapse after their departure before he made his own; and he sat in Hinkler's cockpit all night to guard the aeroplane whilst Bert rested. (Hinkler also brought Bill a letter from his wife.) The last part of Hinkler's flight, over the Timor Sea to Darwin, was made on February 22nd 1928. He landed just as the sun was setting. He had almost halved the time of the Smiths' Vimy in 1919. He then made a triumphal tour around Australia, and was awarded £2000 by the Australian government. His flying time was 128 hours over fifteen and a half days, for a journey of 11,000 miles. His flight marked a watershed on the map of aviation.

Sadly, on January 7th 1933, Hinkler died attempting to fly again to Australia and beat the then-existing record set by C.W.A. Scott in April 1932. He took off from Hayes in the Canadian-registered D.H. 80A Puss Moth, CF-APK, which he had flown from Canada in December 1931 making a crossing of the South Atlantic on the way. That night, Bert flew into a mountain in the Apennines, in a snow-storm. The wreckage of his 'plane, and his body, were not found until April.

In 1931, Charles Grey of *The Aeroplane* (truly an *éminence grise* of aviation) had written ' . . . if I were asked who is the best British aviator I should say without hesitation, — "Bert Hinkler." ' (Australians might have preferred him to say best Commonwealth aviator.)

An obituary of Hinkler by T. Stanhope Sprigg, in the April 1933 issue of *Air and Airways,* which he edited, said: ' . . . he who had so often shown himself superlative master of the air at last fell victim to it, to join that gallant band who died with their feet upon the rudder-bar.'

Hinkler's house 'Mon Repos' at Shorling, Southampton, has now been taken to pieces, shipped to Australia, and re-built in his home town of Bundaberg — a remarkable tribute to a great man. •

25

30/80h.p. "CIRRUS" AERO ENGINES

have been supplied to :—
THE BRITISH AIR MINISTRY.
25 DIFFERENT COUNTRIES.
30 LIGHT AEROPLANE CLUBS.
11 FOREIGN AIRCRAFT CONSTRUCTORS,
etc., etc

are fitted in the :—
D.H. "MOTH,"
AVRO "AVIAN,"
WESTLAND "WIDGEON,"
BLACKBURN "BLUEBIRD,"
SHORT "MUSSEL" (Light Seaplane),
etc., etc.

Manufactured by
THE PIONEERS OF 4-CYL-IN-LINE AIR-COOLED LIGHT AEROPLANE ENGINES.

A.D.C. AIRCRAFT, LTD.,

REGENT HOUSE, KINGSWAY, LONDON, W.C.2.

Telephone : HOLBORN 4076.
Telegrams : AIRDISCO, LONDON.

Contractors to the BRITISH AIR MINISTRY and most FOREIGN GOVERNMENTS.
Constructors of "CIRRUS" and "NIMBUS" Aero Engines.
Construotors of "MARTINSYDE" Types of Aircraft.

WORKS & AERODROME
CROYDON, SURREY.

25. Advertisement, in the 'Programme of Flying' for the ninth Royal Air Force Display, Hendon, 1928, for A.D.C. Cirrus engines as fitted in Hinkler's Avian. Note, in bottom right-hand corner: 'Works and Aerodrome/Croydon, Surrey'.

26. The restored Avian, G-EBOV, in Queensland Museum. The Baby can also be seen, on the extreme left.

26

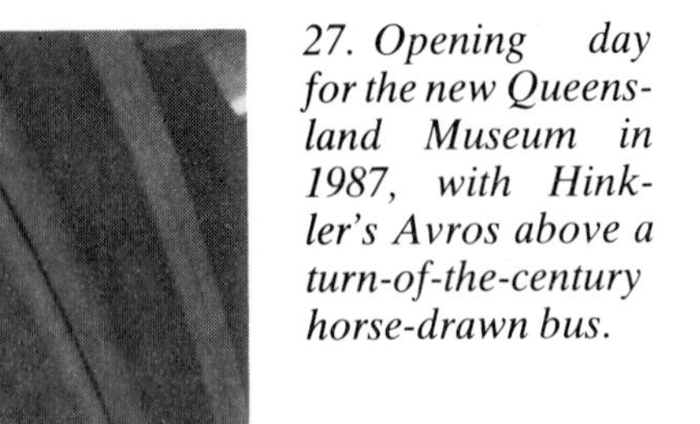

27. *Opening day for the new Queensland Museum in 1987, with Hinkler's Avros above a turn-of-the-century horse-drawn bus.*

28

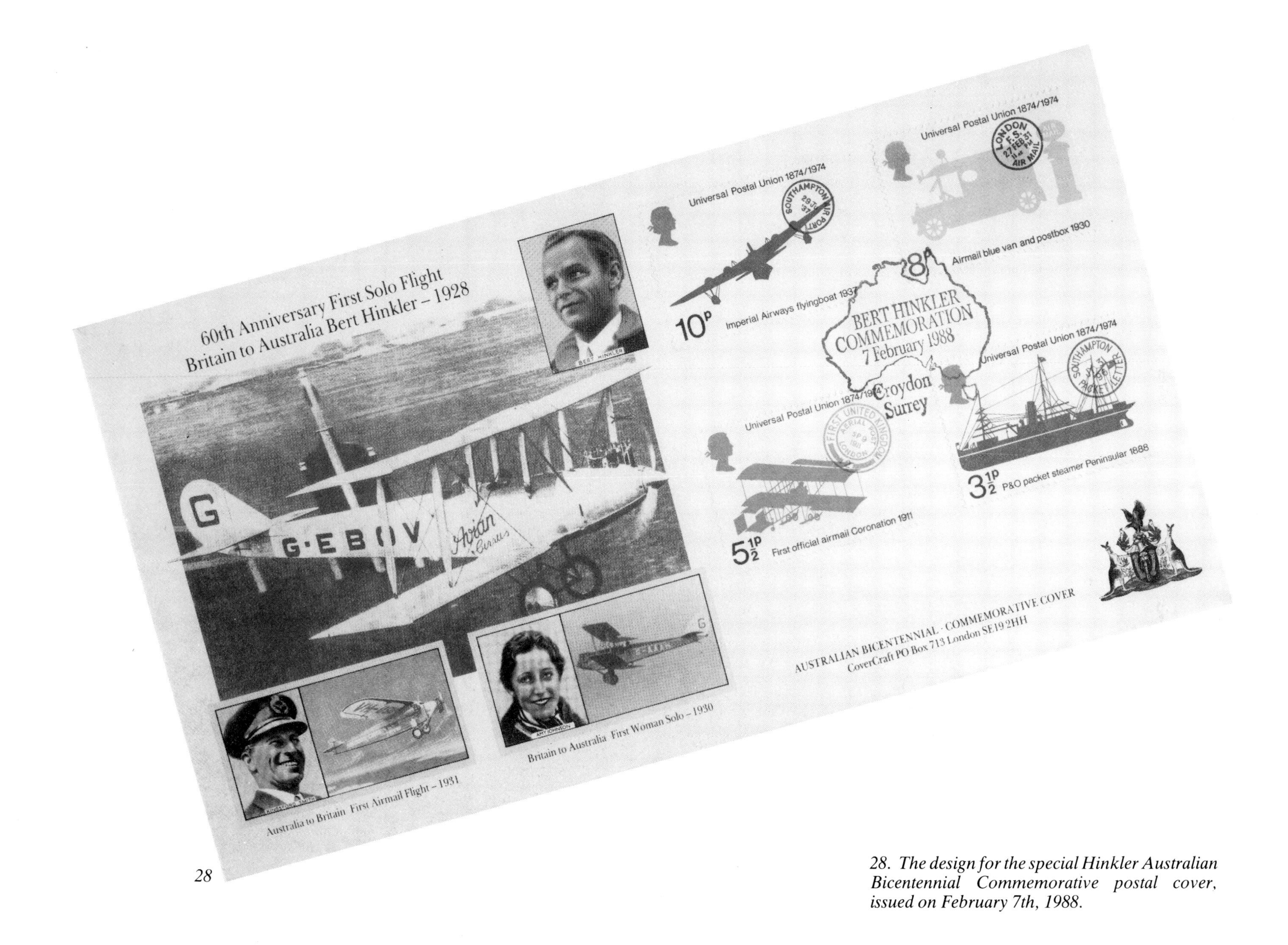

28. The design for the special Hinkler Australian Bicentennial Commemorative postal cover, issued on February 7th, 1988.

RICH YOUNG MAN'S AMAZING FLIGHT.

2,000 MILES DASH ALONE.

"I'm Going to Australia."

3 A.M. START.

ROSS FRANCE IN A DAY.

NE of the most audacious fights ever attempted is now in progress.

At three o'clock yesterday morning, as exclusively nced in the later editions of *The Daily Mail*, Mr. Francis chester, a rich young New Zealander, set out from Croydon rome in an attempt to fly alone to Australia.

So closely secret had he kept the whole scheme that his in n became known only a few minutes before he left. A hanic who was helping to prepare the aeroplane jocularly ked, "Going to Australia, aren't you?" and received n Mr. Chichester the unexpected answer, "Yes."

With a "Thanks, cheerio," to the mechanic he entered machine and away it climbed into the brilliantly moonlit

He has been a pilot for only three months.

He reached Lyons, France, at 10.22 a.m., and resumed his two hours later.

29

29. Daily Mail *coverage of Chichester's departure from Croydon. He left at 2.30am on Friday December 20th, 1929.*

FRANCIS CHICHESTER — RICH YOUNG MAN — LATER ROUND-THE-WORLD YACHTSMAN — FLIES FROM CROYDON TO AUSTRALIA IN 1929

Francis Chichester was knighted after winning the first solo sailing-race across the Atlantic in 1960 in his yacht Gipsy Moth III. In 1965, at the age of 63, he sailed round the world in Gipsy Moth IV. Many years before, however, he had been well-known as a pioneer airman, and although Gipsy Moths II, III and IV were yachts, Chichester's first Gipsy Moth was a D.H.60G Gipsy Moth aircraft, G-AAKK, *Madame Elijah*. Though described above as a rich young New Zealander, Chichester was actually born in Barnstaple, Devon, In 1901, emigrating to New Zealand in 1919, where he made a fortune as an estate agent, having failed to do so as a gold-miner. Returning to Britain in 1929, he learned to fly (he had begun to learn in New Zealand when he had become a partner in an aviation company, but was a 'bad pupil'). He had all along intended to fly back to the Antipodes, and in September he bought the Gipsy Moth for the purpose. His flight to Australia (made with very little preparation) was the first step in a projected flight around the world. He reached Darwin, without major mishap, on January 15th, 1930, after five weeks. His was the second solo flight, and the second light aircraft flight, Britain to Australia. Shipped to New Zealand, the Moth became ZK-AAK and a seaplane. Chichester then made the first solo flight from New Zealand to Australia. His attempted flight Australia-England, west-east, in 1931, ended with a crash in Japan in which he was injured and *Madame Elijah* written-off. He died in 1972. •

30. Madame Elijah *('Gipsy Moth I').*

30

31

31. Southern Cross *on arrival at Croydon, July 10th 1929. The aircraft was a non-standard Fokker F. VIIB/3m, big-winged, and fitted with three 220hp Wright Whirlwind engines and a modified rudder.*

32

Wing-Comdr. Kingsford-Smith.

CHARLES KINGSFORD-SMITH: 'SMITHY'

At the time of his death, the man called by many just 'Smithy' was entitled to be known as Air Commodore Sir Charles Edward Kingsford-Smith. If Bert Hinkler wasn't Australia's greatest airman, then Smithy was. Both were great international aviators, whose lives had far-reaching effects on the history and development of flight. Smithy, indeed, has been called 'the world's greatest aviator'.

He was born in Brisbane on February 9th, 1897, about four years later than Hinkler. His parents were Mr. and Mrs. William Charles Smith, and all seven of their children were given their mother's maiden name, Kingsford, as a middle name. Charles (Chilla to his family) later hyphenated Kingsford-Smith, though not always. His father was a bank manager; but for some six years in Smithy's childhood, took a job with the Canadian Pacific Railway, and the family lived in Canada, returning to Australia to live in Sydney in 1906.

Smithy was a short and slender man, five feet six inches tall. When the First World War began he was seventeen. He wanted to enlist in the army, and was allowed to on his eighteenth birthday. Until that time he had worked as an electrician in the sugar industry. He was sent to Egypt and then France, where he was selected to train as a pilot in the Royal Flying Corps. By the time he was twenty he was teaching flying, had lost all the toes of his left foot after an aerial battle, and won the Military Cross.

After the war he, too, wished to take part in the race to Australia, for the £10,000 prize, with two companions; but the Australian Prime Minister, William Morris Hughes, banned them from the race as too young: a curious decision and one which foreshadowed other official rejections in Smithy's life. He decided to go to America. In

33

33. Southern Cross *outside the hangars at Croydon in 1930. This would be at the time when Smithy had brought her back from her overhaul at the Fokker works in Holland, and was about to fly her to Ireland for the trans-Atlantic trip to Newfoundland, leaving Portmarnock Strand, Dublin on 24th June and arriving at Harbour Grace on the 25th after about thirty-one hours (see also p 26). Note the long grass on the edge of the airfield (in places this was still mown for hay at this period).*

34

34. *Smithy and his crew on July 10th 1930. These are the same men who had been marooned at 'Coffee Royal' earlier in the year. In flying kit, Charles Ulm (left) and Smithy (right) stand between Sir Sefton Brancker (right) and Mr Frederick Montague, Under-Secretary of State for Air (left).*

35. *The whole crew leave* Southern Cross. *With Smith and Ulm, co-pilot, are Harold Litchfield (left) navigator, and Tom McWilliams (right), radio operator. The tall figure with the umbrella on the far right looks like Major Leslie Richard, Chief Aerodrome Officer, Croydon, 1926–1935.*

35

36

36. *The leading engine of* Southern Cross *with the Aerodrome Hotel at Croydon as a back-drop.* Southern Cross *was purchased by the Australian government after Smithy's last flight in her (see p 25) and is now preserved at Brisbane Airport.*

Hollywood, he became a stunt flier for Universal, and then joined a flying circus. When the proprietor decamped with the takings, leaving the fliers with nothing, he decided to return to Australia, which he did at the beginning of 1921. He got a job with Digger's Aviation Company, formed by an old R.F.C. friend, Lionel Lee, and then with West Australian Airways. Here he met another pilot, Keith Anderson, with whom he next went into a sheep-trucking business to raise money for a planned trans-Pacific flight. In 1925 they sold up, bought two Bristol aircraft, and flew them from Perth to Sydney to find a sponsor for their projected flight. First, however, Smithy met a man called Charles Ulm, who was to be his major partner in the future. Ulm persuaded Smithy that a round-Australia record flight would be a good way of arousing interest in, and support for, the bigger enterprise; and it was Ulm who flew with Smithy on this venture. They completed the tour in ten days, five and a half hours, easily a new record, and were welcomed back to Sydney by 50,000 people — and the Premier of New South Wales, who promised financial support. Although this turned out to have a limit of £3,000, not nearly what they needed, Smithy, Ulm and Anderson nevertheless set sail for the USA to find an aircraft and fly back. They acquired a Fokker tri-motored aeroplane built for an explorer, Hubert Wilkins, who had planned to fly over the North Pole in it. They bought it for £3,000 (half down), named it *Southern Cross* after the constellation visible only in the southern hemisphere, and re-engined it with three Wright Whirlwinds. They needed more money before they could make their flight, however, and during their prolonged search for sponsorship Anderson decided he had had enough and went home to get married. Smithy and Ulm were on the point of selling *Southern Cross* when they were introduced to a shipping millionaire who offered to be their backer. They made the flight, in the teeth of bad weather, between May 31st and June 9th 1928, in eighty-three and a half hours for 7,389 miles.

Smithy and Ulm then formed a company called Australian National Airlines, and set out to form an Australian internal airway system. More external flights, however, were needed to maintain what would now be called a high profile, and they next made the first flight over the treacherous Tasman Sea to New Zealand, in September 1928.

It was in July 1929 that Smithy first flew into Croydon Airport — in *Southern Cross*. His successful flight, the first from Australia to England made by Australians, was shadowed by an abortive earlier start which ended in tragedy: Smithy, with Charles Ulm, Tom McWilliams (navigator) and Harold Litchfield (wireless operator) had left Richmond Aerodrome, Sydney, on March 31st. Through an accumulation of misfortunes, they became lost on the way to Wyndham, their first destination, ran out of fuel, and had to land on a desolate mud flat, subsequently to be known as 'Coffee Royal' because of the crew's only available refreshment: half a bottle of brandy and some cold coffee which they mixed and called Coffee Royal. During a search for them (they were located after twelve days) Smithy's old friend and original partner Keith Anderson, and Bob Hitchcock (another old associate) crashed and were killed in the Westland Widgeon III *Kookaburra*, a small aircraft. (When found, and refuelled, *Southern Cross* took part in the search for *Kookaburra*). At the time there were suggestions that the forced landing and search had been engineered by Smithy for publicity purposes, but an official enquiry cleared him. The flight was re-started from Sydney on June 25th, and this time reached Croydon on July 10th, after thirteen days, about the same length of time they were marooned at Coffee Royal. Smithy and his crew returned to Australia by sea whilst *Southern Cross* was overhauled in Holland by the Fokker Company; Smith returning in 1930 to collect her, and coming again to Croydon before leaving for Ireland, from where he flew her to Newfoundland in thirty-one hours. He then flew her across North America to California, completing the circumnavigation of the globe begun with the Pacific flight, before ▶

38

37

37. *Smithy's Avro Ten,* Southern Star, *VH-UMG at Croydon on arrival with the Christmas air mail, December 16th 1931. The inscription on the fuselage had also been borne by the aircraft* Southern Sun *which started the flight and crashed at Alor Star on November 26th. Presumably it was painted on* Southern Star *between that date and Smithy's leaving Darwin on December 3rd.* 38. *One piece of mail, to a famous addressee, carried among the 50,000 letters and cards of the first all-Australian air mail.*

39

39. *'Father Christmas! Air Commodore Kingsford-Smith, M.C., A.F.C., R.A.A.F.', was the original caption to this picture in* Flight, *December 25th, 1931.*

40

40. *Discharging the cargo of Christmas mail from Australia and New Zealand into Imperial Airways' carts. The Croydon Airport terminal building can be seen in the background.*

Smithy's last visit to Croydon.

41. Lady Southern Cross *at Croydon, either before the October 20th take-off for the attempt on the England–Australia record set by C.W.A. Scott and T. Campbell Black in the 'MacRobertson' race (see p 63) or, probably, on the return for repairs, after damage at Brindisi, to Croydon on October 22nd.*

42. *The Lockheed 8D Altair, G-ADUS (formerly VH-USB)* Lady Southern Cross *in the air. The final departure from England on November 6th was the beginning of Smithy's last flight. After November 8th* Lady Southern Cross, *Smithy, and his co-pilot, John Pethybridge, were never seen again — except that part of the aircraft's undercarriage was washed ashore on an island near Burma, two years later.*

41

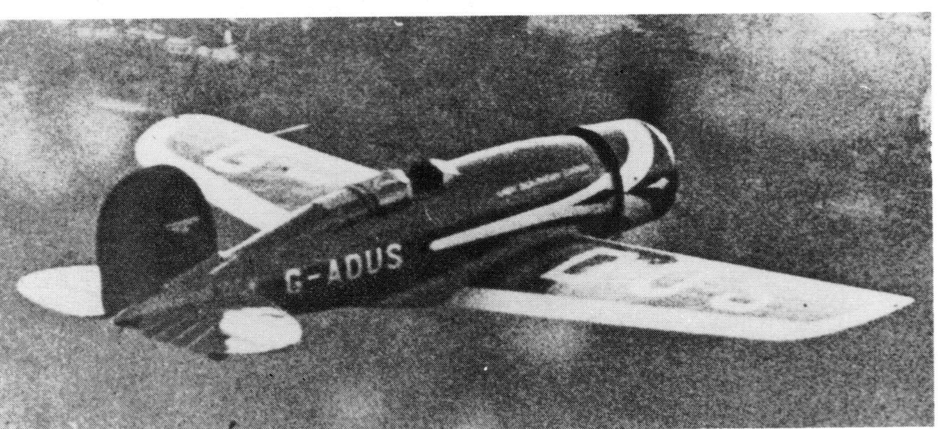

42

before having her shipped home after another overhaul.

In 1930, Smithy beat Hinkler's record from England to Australia in a light aircraft, leaving Heston Aerodrome, north of London, on October 9th, and arriving at Darwin just under ten days later. The aircraft was an Avro 616 Sports Avian IV A, G-ABCF, *Southern Cross Junior*. Its engine, however, was a 120hp Gipsy II, as against Hinkler's 80hp Cirrus II.

In between these flights, Smithy and Ulm were building up Australian National Airways, establishing daily services between major cities with a fleet of aircraft all of which were given names beginning with 'Southern'. It was after Smithy's unsuccessful flight in *Southern Cross Minor* (see p 8) that he was asked by the Australian government to transport a special Christmas air mail — the first all-Australian air mail — to England, with a hint that this would be the forerunner of a regular service for which A.N.A. would have a contract. The mail left Sydney on November 20th in *Southern Sun*, VH-UNA, an Avro 618 Ten (Ten because it was a ten-seater) based, under licence, on the Fokker F.VIIB/3m, of which *Southern Cross* was an example. The pilot was 'Scotty' Allan. Allan, however, crashed at Alor Star near Singapore. Smithy, who had not intended to make this air mail flight himself because of work pressure, set out with another Avro Ten, *Southern Star*, VH-UMG; rescued crew and mail from *Southern Sun*, and all flew off to England, arriving at Croydon on December 16th, having taken thirteen days from Darwin. They left again from Croydon on 8th January 1932, with 700 pounds of mail for Australia, reaching Darwin eleven days later. It was all a great blow, therefore, when the Australian government, after tenders, gave the Australia–England air mail contract to Q.A.N.T.A.S. (see p 52); and soon after A.N.A. was wound up. Smithy sold all the aircraft except *Southern Cross*. Around this time he married a Melbourne girl called Mary Powell, although there were rumours that he had married before, in his sheep-trucking days. It was at this time, too, that he was given his knighthood by King George V (to the displeasure of some fellow-countrymen). Smithy now toured the country giving joy-rides in *Southern Cross*.

In 1933 he again broke the England–Australia record, by then held by C.W.A. Scott (see p. 62), flying a Percival Gull Four, G-ACJV, *Miss Southern Cross* from Lympne to Wyndham in seven days five hours, from October 4th to October 11th.

His last major flight in *Southern Cross* was an unfortunate one. It was an attempt to make a special historic philatelic flight to New Zealand with air mail, including some from King George, before retiring the ageing aircraft. Bad weather, and one engine going out of action, necessitated the dropping of the mail in the sea, and a return to Sydney. Following this he sold *Southern Cross* to the Australian government in 1935.

Smithy was last at Croydon in October 1935. At thirty-eight he wanted one more long-distance success before he was forty. He determined to beat the Scott and Campbell-Black record from England to Australia set in the Comet racer G-ACSS (see p 54). The aircraft was his Lockheed Altair, *Lady Southern Cross*, G-ADUS. John Pethybridge was his co-pilot. They took off from Croydon on October 20th 1935, but had to return for repairs after damage at Brindisi. On November 6th *Lady Southern Cross* left England via Lympne. She reached Singapore; but, after leaving on November 8th, was never seen again. Smithy, too, died with his feet on the rudder-bar. •

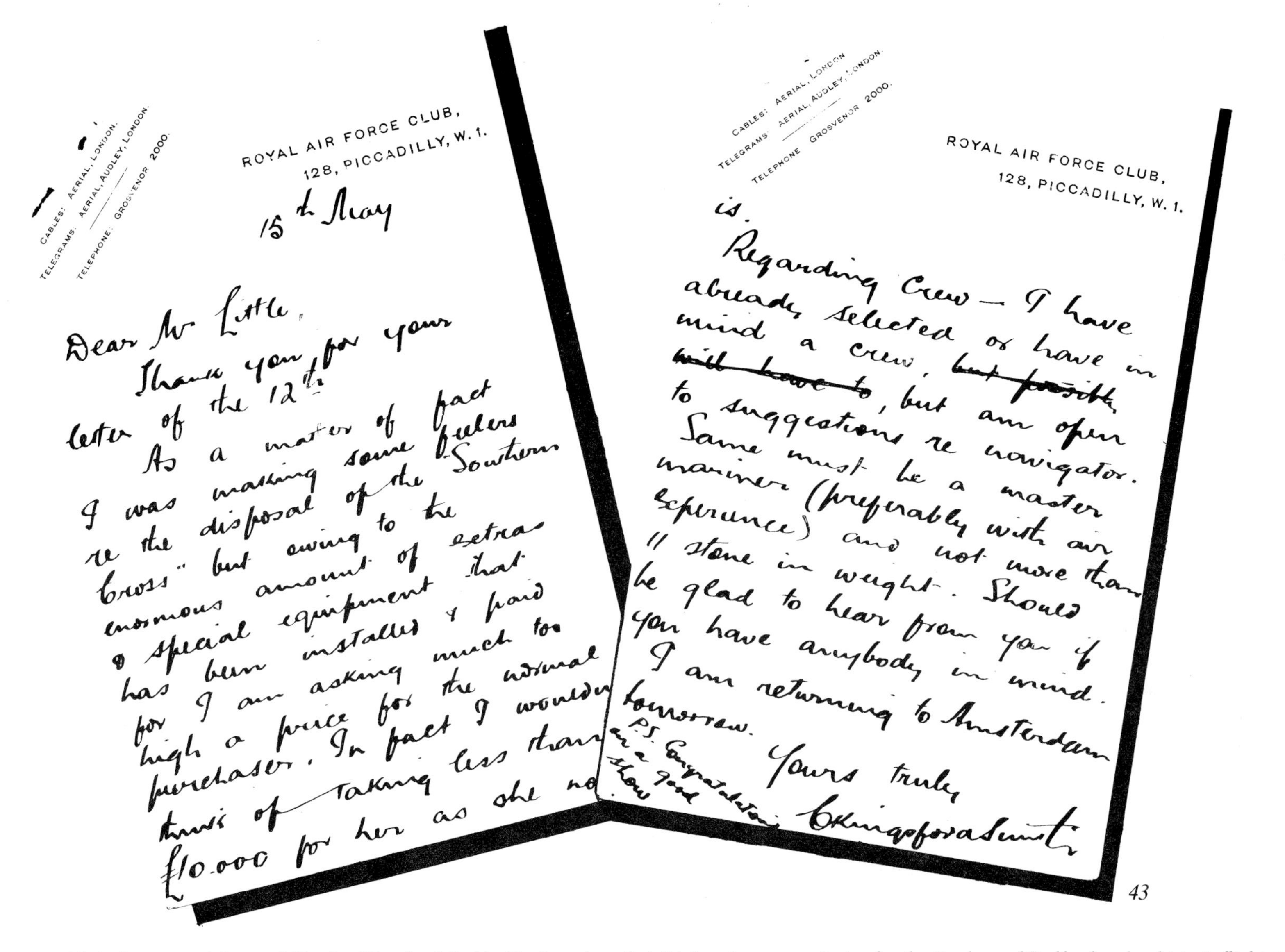

ROYAL AIR FORCE CLUB,
128, PICCADILLY, W. 1.

CABLES: AERIAL, LONDON.
TELEGRAMS: AERIAL, AUDLEY, LONDON.
TELEPHONE: GROSVENOR 2000.

15th May

Dear Mr Little,

Thank you for your letter of the 12th.

As a matter of fact I was making some feelers re the disposal of the "Southern Cross" but owing to the enormous amount of extras & special equipment that has been installed & paid for I am asking much too high a price for the normal purchaser. In fact I wouldn't think of taking less than £10.000 for her as she now is.

Regarding crew — I have already selected or have in mind a crew, ~~but possibly~~ ~~will have to~~, but am open to suggestions re navigator. Same must be a master mariner (preferably with air experience) and not more than 11 stone in weight. Should be glad to hear from you if you have anybody in mind.

I am returning to Amsterdam tomorrow.

Yours truly
C Kingsford Smith

P.S. Congratulations on a good show.

43

43. *A hitherto unpublished autograph letter of Charles Kingsford-Smith. The letter is to Bob Little, who was navigator for the Duchess of Bedford on her historic flights to India (1929) and Cape Town (1930). The year of the letter must be 1930, and it belongs to the period between Smithy's collecting* Southern Cross *from Holland and flying her across the Atlantic. Probably Bob Little was inquiring about purchasing* Southern Cross *on behalf of the Duchess. It is interesting to note that (a) Smithy was considering the sale of his 'Old Bus', but perhaps not until he had completed his circumnavigation of the globe; (b) the value he places on it is the same as that declared at the 'Coffee Royal' inquiry in 1929 (the final sale to the Australian government in July 1935 was for the £3,000 he had originally paid); and (c) it looks as though the position of navigator on the forthcoming flight was not finalised, and he appears to be hinting that Bob might like the job. The 'ps' must refer to the Cape Town flight which had finished back at Croydon on April 19th 1930.*

44. Oarangi *outside a hangar at Croydon with Harold Piper and Cyril Kay.* *44*

TWO NEW ZEALANDERS FLY FROM CROYDON TO DARWIN IN A CROYDON-BUILT AIRCRAFT — FIRST CABIN MONOPLANE TO MAKE THE JOURNEY, 1930

In February 1930 two R.A.F. Flying Officers, Harold Piper and Cyril Kay, both of No. 26 Squadron, took three months' leave. Both were New Zealanders, and they had been impressed by Hinkler's flight. It occured to them that a flight to Australia might be a quick way of getting home for a visit (they would have to go by sea from Australia to New Zealand, though, because at that time 'the sea passage was not allowed to be flown by small land machines' (*Flight* 14/2/30)). They also hoped to knock some time off Hinkler's record. Piper purchased for the purpose an aircraft made by the Desoutter Company at Croydon Aerodrome, a Mk I Desoutter G-AATI, fitted with a Cirrus Hermes 105hp engine, manufactured by the Aircraft Disposal Company, also of Croydon. He named the Desoutter *Oarangi*. Their place of departure, too, was Croydon, on February 19th.

They did not beat Hinkler's record, largely due to three emergency landings, two with the engine overheating: the first near Jask, on the Persian Gulf, when a piston disintegrated, and the second near Akyab, Burma. In each case the trouble started over water, increasing the hazard. At Akyab they had to wait three weeks for spares to reach them. This accounted for about half the time that had elapsed when they reached Port Darwin on March 23rd. Theirs was the first flight to Australia in a light cabinned-aircraft; the first, as *Flight* said at the time: 'carried out in comfort'. They flew *Oarangi* to Sydney and then returned home to New Zealand by sea. The Desoutter went to New Zealand too, and became ZK-ACJ, remaining in use for twenty years until written-off in 1950. Cyril Kay later flew in the 1934 'MacRobertson' race to Australia with J.D. Hewett, coming fifth with the D.H. 89 Dragon Rapide ZK-ACO *Tainui* in just under thirteen days, nineteen hours.

The Desoutter Aircraft Co. Ltd. was formed by Marcel Desoutter in 1929, with its works at Croydon in former National Aircraft Factory hangars. Forty-one monoplanes were built there, of which nineteen were for National Flying Services, which ran a nation-wide chain of flying clubs. Another Desoutter to make a long-distance flight was G-AAPY, which Charles B. Wilson, pilot for the *Daily Mail*, flew 5,500 miles to Baghdad and back in the flying-time of sixty-two hours, in June 1930. A third was G-ABOM, flown by Harold Jeffery and Harold Jenkins (both Australians), from Croydon or Heston to Darwin in six weeks in 1931-32, perhaps the first 'tourist' flight to Australia. The Desoutter stayed in Australia as VH-UEE, *Miss Flinders*, and was preserved after thirty years of flying there. ●

'AMY, WONDERFUL AMY' — FIRST WOMAN TO FLY SOLO TO AUSTRALIA, FROM CROYDON, MAY 1930

No flier in the 1930s caught the public imagination quite like Amy Johnson did. 'The typist who flew to Australia' is how many people at the time would have described her.

Amy was born in Hull, Yorkshire, on July 1st, 1903, in a terraced house. She was the first born of four daughters. Her father, John William Johnson, known as Will, worked in the family fish-marketing business of Johnson, Knudtzon and Co., founded by his Danish father, Anders Jorgensen, who came to England and changed his name to Johnson. Her mother, who had been Amy Hodge, was always known as 'Ciss'. In 1914 Amy's father succeeded his father as head of the business.

The 'little typist' was not really the true image of Amy; she gained a B.A. degree from Sheffield University and worked at a number of occupations before taking up flying, including copywriting for an advertising agency in Hull.

When she came to London in 1927 her first job was in the Peter Jones department store; she then went to work for a solicitor acquaintance of her father's (she did have to start in his office as a typist). Her leaving Hull had partly to do with a love affair, over which there had been family problems (he was a Swiss Catholic, and her mother was a staunch Methodist). It was when this affair finally broke up that Amy began flying. One of her motives was probably to shock her ex-lover by turning to this dangerous pastime.

Her first flight had been back in 1926, when she and her next-but-one sister, Molly, had gone up for a joy-ride (probably in an Avro 536) when Surrey Flying Services (of Croydon Aerodrome) were visiting Hull. In April 1928, in one of her last letters to 'Franz' (not his real name) she mentioned having seen the film *Wings,* about the First World War in the air, which revived her interest in flight; and then making a trip to Hendon, where she gatecrashed the London Aeroplane Club and got into conversation with a pilot who told her she could join the club for £3.3.0 (three guineas) and learn to fly for thirty shillings per hour. It was not until September that there was a vacancy, however. By that time she had heard that 'Franz' had married. She wrote to him no more, but was deeply scarred. She became more than ever determined to learn to fly. If she killed herself — well, she hadn't much to lose. At one time, she told a friend (Jimmy Martin, later Sir James and inventor of the jet-plane ejector seat), she considered a deliberate crash, but had abandoned the idea because she came to love flying so much.

Amy's first flying lesson was with Captain F.R. Matthews, Chief Instructor of the London Aeroplane Club. Two years later both he and this new pupil were to fly to Australia; but she did it four months before he did. 1929 was the year when she both bought a car (in April) and gained her 'A' pilot's licence (in July) with a total flying time of nineteen hours (she soon sold her car again to get the money to go on flying). ▶

45

45. Amy in her Sidcot flying suit, probably before the take-off for Australia.

O.A. Form 10.

AIR MINISTRY—CIVIL AVIATION.

No. 12079

Date 4-5-30

Aerodrome.

Unit

Account for services rendered at Croydon

Name of Pilot Miss. A. Johnson

Address

Type and particulars of machine Moth GAAAH

	AA £ s. d.	A £ s. d.	B £ s. d.	C £ s. d.	D £ s. d.	£ s. d.
Landing fees		2 6				2 6
Housing fees, 8 hrs. or less...						
„ „ 24 „ „						
„ „ Monthly rates...						
„ „ Special Agreement*						
Total charges for housing and landing...						2 6

Class of Machine. (For details, see A.M.W.O. 169/27 para. 2 (iii).)

*For use at Civil Aerodromes.

Other charges (in detail, voucher numbers being quoted where necessary)—

47

AIR TAXIS LIMITED
STAG LANE AERODROME
EDGWARE - LONDON - N.W.

M Miss Amy Johnson.,

24th April 1930

To

One Gipsy Moth Aeroplane G AAAH 600 0 0

No 208 RECEIVED THE S... £600-0-0
FOR AIR TAXIS LIMITED. STAG LANE AERODROME, EDGWARE.
By George Camp...
With Compliments

46

48

48. Amy poses beside Jason *for the cameraman on the morning of May 5th 1930. The Croydon terminal building can be seen in the background.*

Also, that year, Amy met a man who was to become a great stabilising factor in her life, and on whom she came to lean heavily: 'Jack' (really Charles) Humphreys, chief ground engineer at the London Aeroplane Club. In December she got her ground engineer's 'C' licence (for a while she was the only woman in the world to possess such a thing). She decided she needed a spectacular exploit to secure a career in aviation.

It was around the turn of the year that she conceived the idea of flying to Australia, probably because it was the major flight, other than the trans-Atlantic crossing — for which she would have needed much more experience — that no woman had yet tried. She acquired her pilot's 'B' licence (needing a hundred hours solo and a 200-mile flight), and her ground engineer's 'A' licence. She began to canvass support for her flight, and gained the help of Sir Sefton Brancker in persuading Lord Wakefield to back the flight, as he had done for Cobham.

On April 24th 1930 Amy bought a second-hand D.H. 60G Gipsy Moth, G-AAAH, which she named *Jason* after the brand name of her father's firm. On Sunday 4th May she flew it from Stag Lane to Croydon. Her father had come south to see her off for Australia — she intended to leave the next day at sunrise — and both spent the night in the Aerodrome Hotel. Will Johnson woke his daughter next morning after he himself had been called. Sunrise was at about 4.30am. Amy, asked how she felt, said: 'Lousy. I couldn't sleep for the traffic [in Purley Way]'. Only her father and a few friends were there to see Amy off, but they included Jack Humphreys and Jimmy Martin. A few pressmen and one photographer turned up. She posed for him. As she was about to leave she discovered a leaking petrol pipe, and her departure was delayed for several hours. It was at about 7.30am that she was again ready to get away, and then it took two attempts to get the heavily-laden *Jason* off the ground; which she achieved at 7.45am. She took a spare airscrew, a parachute, lent by the Irving Company; a fire extinguisher, lent by Pyrene; and a dressing-gown, lent by her mother, to whom she had written: 'I'm taking every precaution, you may be sure. I am getting heaps of things for nothing — watches, clocks, alarm clocks, engine parts, new wheels, etc. etc. It's great fun.' At the end of the second leg of the flight, Vienna-Constantinople, she found waiting for her a cablegram — believed to be the only message she received there — reading 'Best luck and wishes — Franz'. This, it seems, increased, rather than alleviated, her feeling of homesickness and loneliness at this stage. She pressed on, however.

As the flight progressed, the press began to get more and more interested. At Karachi she had beaten ▶

46/47. (Opposite) Two previously unpublished documents: 46 (below): The receipt for £600 paid by Amy to Air Taxis Ltd. for Jason, *eleven days before the flight to Australia began. 47 (above): Amy's landing fee of half a crown (two shillings and sixpence) for bringing* Jason *in to Croydon Airport on the day before she flew off into history.*

49

Photo
Taken near our workshop gate as fixing the rear of plane to the Motor Truck to be taken to the Race course.
I am near the propellor supporting the front.
You are standing towards the rear of the plane with an umbrellor having a look at the fixing of the tail to the truck.

49. Jason *at Insein, five miles north of Rangoon. Amy Johnson is beneath the farthest umbrella on the left. Amy had intended to land on Rangoon racecourse, for which arrangements had been made, there being no airfield there. However, in torrential rain, she could not find it, and put down, with the last of her fuel, on the best place she could, which proved to be the playing field of the Technical Institute at Insein. Here, the field being too small, she ran* Jason *into a ditch 'into which he buried his head and came to a standstill . . . I cried like a baby', she wrote later.* Jason *had a ripped tyre, damage to undercarriage and a wing, and a broken propeller. He was rescued from the ditch and carried to the shelter of nearby trees. 'This done, I went to bed and refused to be disturbed even for dinner.' Next day, the Head of the Institute, a Mr. Shaw, placed his pupils' services at Amy's disposal. They fitted the spare propeller and repaired the rest of the damage.* Jason *was towed backwards behind the local fire engine to Rangoon (take-off from the field being impossible) at five m.p.h. Here she tested the machine in the air before taking-off for Bangkok on 16th May. Her three-day delay had cost her her two-day lead over Hinkler.*

50

50. V.N. Pal, one of the Insein Technical Institute students who helped Amy with her propeller. It was he who sent Amy both photographs reproduced on this page. On the back of the photo shown above he wrote the inscription reproduced below it: 'Taken near our workshop gate [as?] fixing the rear of plane to the motor truck to be taken to the Race Course. I am near the propeller supporting the front. You are standing towards the rear of the plane with an umbrellor [sic] having a look at the fixing of the tail to the truck'. On the photograph of himself, printed on a postcard, he signed the front 'Cowboy Pal' and on the back wrote: 'With best Compliments and Sincerest wishes for a Bon-Voyage. From V.N. Pal, Mechanical Student, Govt: Technical: Inst: INSEIN Rangoon, (Burma); and addressed it (it was not posted as a separate item): Miss Amy Johnson, Aviatrix. (Flight — England — to Australia).'

51. Arrival: On May 24th 1930, after 9,960 miles and nineteen and a half days, Amy lands Jason *at Port Darwin. More than two hundred telegrams and cables awaited her here.* *51*

Bert Hinkler's record that far, but at Rangoon she ran *Jason* into a ditch and was delayed for three days. Here she received the unwelcome news that Jack Humphreys was in hospital, after an accident at Stag Lane Aerodrome, with a badly-broken arm which had been struck by a propeller. At the same time she began to receive the first of the flood of congratulatory messages; and the first of the business and publicity propositions. At Sourabaya her engine was overhauled and a third airscrew (the one she had carried from Croydon as a spare was put on at Rangoon) was fitted. Then there was delay from magneto trouble. It was clear by this time that she would not beat Hinkler's record to Darwin. At nearly the end of the flight there was an alarm, when she could not find the aerodrome on Timor, and landed away from civilisation; and the headlines on May 23rd read: 'Flying Girl Missing'. But she was near a native village, and not so far from the aerodrome as she thought, and she was able, with help, to get *Jason* off again to the airfield at Atamboea for the last leg, over the Timor Sea; five hundred shark-infested miles. She reached Darwin at 3.30pm on 24th May, the first woman to fly solo from Britain to Australia; completing the process of becoming a world heroine in nineteen and a half days.

On the tour of Australia which followed, she made a bad landing at Brisbane and damaged *Jason*. For the rest of her tour she was a passenger. From Brisbane to Sydney she was flown in Kingsford-Smith's *Southern Sun,* the aircraft which later crashed at Alor Star with the all-Australian air mail (see p 25). The pilot was Charles Ulm. The co-pilot was James Allan Mollison, with whom she danced at a ball that evening.

Her return to England was by sea, and then by Imperial Airways airliner to Croydon from Vienna on August 4th. Her welcome there was tumultuous, and there was a twelve-mile procession to the Grosvenor House Hotel where she and her family were to stay. Many celebrations followed. Amy was subjected to much pressure and her health suffered; but she recovered.

On January 1st 1931 she set out to fly to Peking via Siberia in another Gipsy Moth, G-ABDV, *Jason III,* but the weather proved invincible, and her flight ended near Warsaw. In July she set off again, this time for Tokio in a Puss Moth, G-AAZV, *Jason II*. Jack Humphreys went with her. They flew to Tokio and back in seventeen days. Whilst there they visited Francis Chichester in hospital after his seaplane crashed (see p. 19). Next summer they were going to fly round the world; but at Christmas she collapsed and underwent surgery. To convalesce she went on a cruise to Cape Town. There she again met Jim Mollison, who had just concluded a solo flight from England. They were married in July. Their marriage was much publicised, but ultimately unhappy.

In 1932 Amy flew another Puss Moth, G-ACAB, *Desert Cloud,* to Cape Town and back; returning to Croydon on December 18th having beaten Jim's record on the way out, and setting a new record on the way back. Jim and Amy's flights together were not too successful; their attempt on the world long-distance record, in the D.H. Dragon, G-ACCV, *Seafarer,* failed (though they did fly the Atlantic) and they had to drop out of the 'MacRobertson' race in their D.H. Comet racer *Black Magic* though they established new records to Baghdad and Karachi. In May 1936 Amy set new records to the Cape and back in a Percival Gull Six, G-ADZO.

In February 1938 the Mollisons were divorced. When war broke out in 1939 Amy joined the Air Transport Auxiliary, ferrying aircraft. She lost her life in the Thames Estuary, off-course in an Airspeed Oxford aircraft, on January 5th 1941, in circumstances which are still, in 1988, being debated. ●

52

52. *A dense crowd surrounds* Jason *in Australia, probably at Darwin (but possibly at Longreach, or Toowomba, on Amy's Australian tour before she crash-landed at Brisbane).*

53

53. Amy Johnson above Brisbane River on May 29th 1930. This was the last time she was to fly Jason *in Australia.*

54. Jason *on his back after Amy made a bad landing at Brisbane. She overshot the aerodrome, hit the perimeter fence, and overturned in a field beyond it. Amy was not hurt, though much shaken, and only one or two of her public engagements were cancelled. Major Hereward de Havilland, Managing Director of the Australian branch of de Havilland's, himself flew from Melbourne with spares to repair* Jason, *after which the aircraft was crated-up and returned to England by sea, and was waiting at Croydon for Amy on her triumphant return on August 4th.*

54

55

55. After the Brisbane crash, Amy flew in Australia as a passenger. It was as a result of this that her first meeting with Jim Mollison occurred, when Charles Ulm, with Mollison as co-pilot, flew Amy from Brisbane to Sydney in Southern Sun. *Here, however, she appears to be boarding Major de Havilland's six-seater D.H.75 Hawk Moth, G-AAFX, later VH-UNW, in which she was flown on the rest of her tour after Sydney.*

56

56. From Sydney, Amy was flown to Melbourne. The original caption to this photograph, when published in Australia, read: 'One of the biggest crowds that ever thronged Swanston St., cheered Miss Amy Johnson as she arrived at the Melbourne Town Hall. In the city proper, her car had almost to plough through close-packed thousands'. Amy left Australia on July 5th, aboard a P & O liner, Naldera, *by courtesy of Lord Inchcape, P & O's Chairman.*

57. A hitherto unpublished photograph of Amy in Cairo (R.A.F. Heliopolis) on her way back to England from Australia.

58. (Below) On August 4th 1930, Amy, aboard an Imperial Airways Argosy, City of Glasgow, *arrived back at Croydon after her Australian adventure three hours late, owing to strong headwinds over Europe. Many thousands of people had waited throughout the day to welcome her home. The reception ceremony had to take place after dark. Here, Amy, seen under flood-lights, shares the platform with (from left to right): Lt. Cmdr. Kenworthy, M.P. for Hull, Sir Sefton Brancker, Lord Wakefield, Ciss Johnson (her mother), and, at the microphone, Lord Thomson, Secretary of State for Air. (Both Thomson and Brancker, within two months, would be dead, killed in the R101 disaster.)*

57

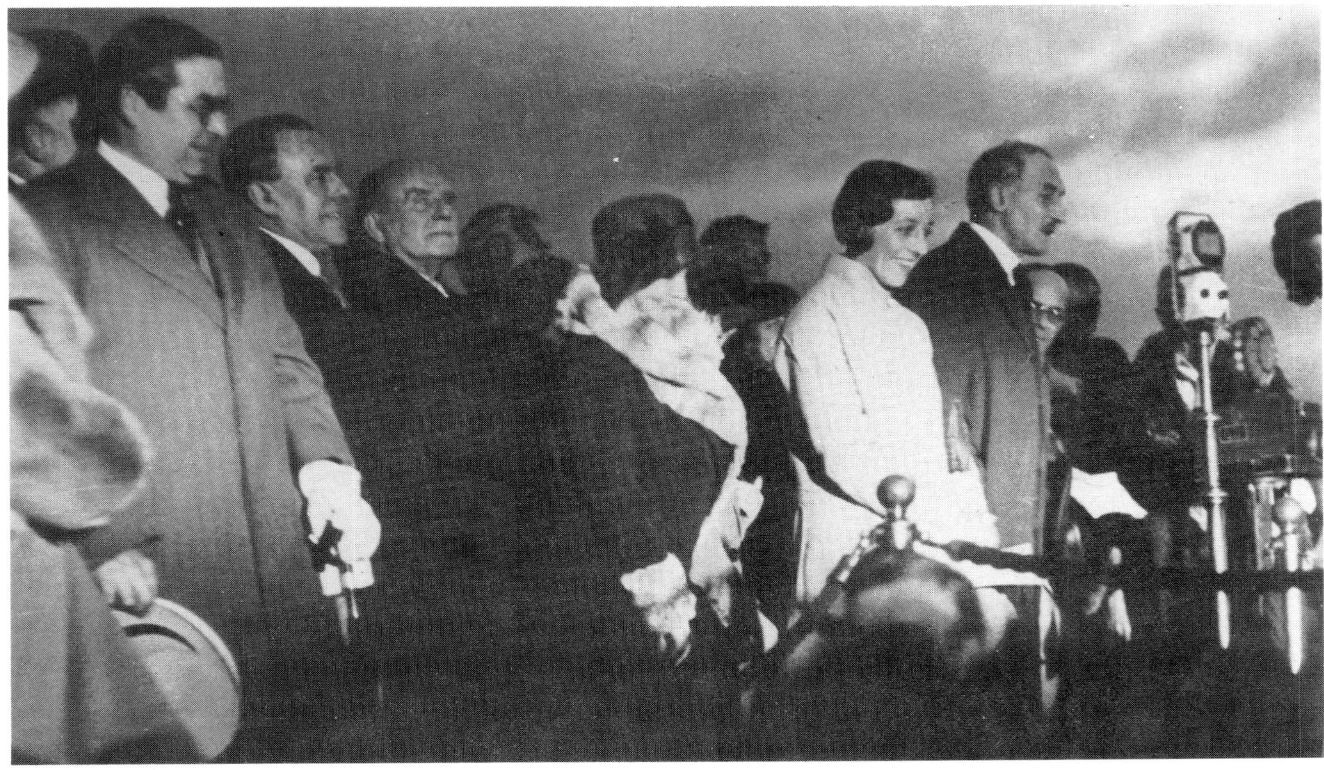

58

59

59. Portrait photograph of Eric Hook.

THE TRAGIC FLIGHT OF ERIC HOOK AND JACK MATTHEWS, 1930

On June 20th 1930, Eric L. Hook and James 'Jack' Matthews set out to lower the record to Australia, as had Amy Johnson a little over a month earlier. They were flying a de Havilland D.H.60M 'Metal Moth' (a metal-fuselaged version of the Gipsy Moth), G-AAWV, *Dryasel*. Neither had been flying long. Hook was a young man with a business in Clapham High Street (he manufactured a product called 'Puncture Proof', an injection method of repairing punctures) and a house in West Wickham, but had been born in Australia, coming to Britain as a music student. Matthews was a mechanic who had worked with Hinkler at Avro's, had also looked after the *Daily Mail's* aircraft, and was well-known at Croydon. Hook was called a 'wealthy young man', but he had apparently sunk all his money in this venture. It was he who had bought the Moth and financed the trip. He had a twenty-two-year-old wife, Dorothy, and two young daughters: Nonie aged four, and Helen, aged two. Mrs. Hook was later to be quoted by the *Daily Herald* as saying: 'My husband's desire to fly to Australia was fired by a film he saw. I think it was "The Sky Hawk". He believed it was his duty to show the way to the youth of England, just as Miss Amy Johnson has done. He went next day to Croydon Aerodrome to arrange for flying lessons . . .' Dorothy Hook had also learned to fly at the same time. Hook and Matthews' final departure, when the flight began, was from Lympne.

A letter from Hook, dated June 2nd, to his mother in Sydney, was quoted in the press later: 'I will get off or bust. The dull leaden skies make me long for Australia. Six days ago I passed all flying tests with the sole object of making a flight to lower the London to Darwin time by a few days. I am not setting out to beat Hinkler [it is difficult to see how he could have done one without the other], but I am using a smaller 'plane and am taking Jack Matthews as a passenger, he having got a licence the same day as myself. Nothing serious is going to happen to me. I can feel success in my bones.'

However, disaster struck on July 3rd after they left Akyab in Burma. A leaking petrol-pipe, and/or an engine penetrated by tropical rain (Matthews is later quoted as giving both as reasons at different times) brought them down from fifty feet to crash into a clump of bamboo in the Yoma mountains. They were unhurt, but clad only in shirts and shorts, and with only 'food tablets' as rations. They set off to walk. They found some fruit to eat on the way. After seven days Hook's strength gave out. He could go no further, but pressed Matthews to go on for help. A day later Jack met some Burmese, but a party sent back to look for Hook could not find him. Matthews was taken on to Prome, some two or three hundred miles north of Rangoon (and about 150 miles from the crash), and cared-for whilst Hook continued to be sought. It was not until July 30th that the finding of a body, seven miles from where Jack had left ►

60

60. A painting by Charles Couper Dickson, doyen of aviation caricaturists, of Eric Hook and Jack Matthews with their aircraft at Croydon, where a number of 'Dickie's' caricatures still hang in the (now renamed) Aerodrome Hotel. At one time a great collection of Charles Dickson's caricatures of everyone of note connected with Croydon Airport was displayed in the Pilots' Bar there. This one is unusual as being a double caricature. It is in the possession of Eric Hook's younger daughter and is believed to be hitherto unpublished.

61

61. Dorothy Hook with Nonie (left) and Helen (right) looking at Eric Hook's photograph whilst seeking news of her husband (a posed newspaper photograph).

him, was reported, and later identified as Eric Hook's. A swollen river had apparently washed him downstream, and jungle beasts had left only a skeleton. Matthews was eventually brought home by the *Daily Herald*. A fund was started for Eric Hook's widow and children. Amy Johnson was reported on August 7th to be giving £100 to this. Her journey home coincided with the search for the lost fliers.

At one time Dorothy Hook was considering trying to complete the flight her husband had died attempting, in his memory; but, wisely, perhaps, stayed with her children instead. •

AIR WIDOW'S LONGING

Extract from

Bradford Daily Telegraph

AIRMAN BURIED.

Mr. Hook's Body Found in Jungle.

RANGOON, Thursday.

The funeral of Mr. Eric L. Hook, the missing airman, who crashed while flying to Australia with Mr. J. Matthews, and whose body has been brought to Prome, 300 miles north-east of Rangoon, took place at Prome to-day.

All the landing officials and residents in the district attended, and soldiers followed the cortege with reversed arms.

Mr. Hook's body was found not far from where Mr. Matthews had left him, and it was evident that the dying man had made a last desperate effort to reach safety and failed.

AMY LEAVES CAIRO.

Miss Amy Johnson concluded her visit to Cairo to-day, when she left for Alexandria in a R.A.F. machine (says Exchange).

She will return to London in an Imperial Airways liner, which will leave Salonica on Sunday. She will reach London next Monday.

TO TRY FLIGHT ON WHICH HUSBAND DIED

"HE FAILED . . . I WANT TO CARRY ON FOR HIM"

MRS. HOOK'S FIGHT

ANY JOB TO AID HER TWO CHILDREN

From Our Special Correspondent
WEST WICKHAM (Kent), Sunday.

"I should like to undertake the flight which my husband died in attempting.

"He failed. I should like to carry on for him."

IN level, unemotional tones Mrs. Hook, the 22-year-old widow of the airman who crashed in the Burmese jungle on his way to Australia, made this statement to me at her home here to-night.

Less than a week ago she was finally convinced of the death of the young husband whom she ran away to marry at the age of 16.

Left to face the world with two little daughters, she gives every thought which she can spare for them to deciding what her husband would wish her to do.

"I am still thinking it out," she said.

CHILDREN FIRST

"If I decide to do the flight it won't be yet. I couldn't leave the children until they are safely established, and I have no money.

"I am not a madcap, and should first have to take six months or so in the workshops, as well as making myself a competent pilot. I have had several lessons."

Then Noni, aged four, and Helen, aged two, came in.

"Without them I should have cracked up," said their mother.

Her immediate thought is to get a job. "I can drive any make of car, and have a mechanical turn of mind," she said. "I have had a little selling experience in my husband's business, and have travelled extensively."

AMY HERE TO-DAY

CHEERED ACROSS EUROPE

Miss Amy Johnson will arrive at Croydon Aerodrome at six o'clock this evening.

She flew to Australia alone, and at first almost unheralded, in spite of countless perils and difficulties.

But to-day sees the climax of a return which has been

a triumphal progress half round the world.

During this week-end she was flying across Europe, having spent Saturday night at Salonika and last night at Vienna.

At Budapest, during a halt on her air journey, Amy was fêted by the Hungarian Air Union and vast crowds of cheering people.

Belgrade and Vienna cheered her, too.

Among those who will welcome her at Croydon to-night are three Cabinet Ministers—Mr. J. H. Thomas, Lord Thomson, and Miss Bondfield.

But the first to greet her will be members of her own family from Hull.

And Hull is preparing a terrific welcome.

The town has gone Amy-mad.

BANKER HURT, WIFE KILLED

From Our Own Correspondent
BORDEAUX, Sunday.

Well known in New York as a director of the Chase National Bank, Mr. Amos L. Beaty was severely injured, and his wife killed, in a motor accident at St. Andre de Cubzac, 12 miles from here.

The body of Mrs. Beaty is being transported to New York.

62

62. Newspaper cuttings from Dorothy Hook's scrapbook, in which the sad news of Eric Hook's death is juxtaposed with the happy news of Amy Johnson's triumphant return to Croydon Airport. A last irony was that mourners at a memorial service for Eric Hook were held up by the procession organised in Amy Johnson's honour on her return.

Mr. F. R. Matthews.

F.R. MATTHEWS, FLYING FROM CROYDON, FIRST PAST THE POST IN AN UNINTENTIONAL RACE TO AUSTRALIA

In the issue of October 10th 1930, *Flight* reported on 'several fresh cases' of 'Antipodes Aeronitis', a 'strange malady which was first reported by Bert Hinkler in 1928 ... On October 5 Flight-Lieut. C.W. Hill of Henlow left Lympne in a D.H. "Gipsy Moth" and hopes to "get it over" some several days sooner than Bert Hinkler did ... The next case is a "double" one, for Major C.E.M. Pickthorne and F/O. C.J. Chabot set out in the latter's D.H. "Puss Moth" from Croydon on October 6, hoping ... to beat both Hill *and* Bert Hinkler. All three have reached Constantinople. A second attack of "flu" has prevented the malady from getting a hold of Wing-Com. Kingsford-Smith, who is at Croydon with his Avro "Avian" [G-ABCF, *Southern Cross Junior*] awaiting events. Meanwhile, Capt. F.R. Matthews — who caught the malady on September 16 (also in a "Puss Moth") — is still suffering from a relapse in Siam, but hopes (as soon as certain repairs are effected) to get over this in a few weeks' time ...' Froude Ridler Matthews (no relation to Jack, but the third 'Matthews' to try the flight — the first was George C. in 1920) was the Chief Instructor at the London Aeroplane Club, who had given Amy Johnson her first flying lesson. His D.H. 80A Puss Moth, G-ABDW, was the first used in an Australian attempt. Chabot and Pickthorne starting three weeks later in *their* Puss Moth got no further than Karachi. Kingsford-Smith, who got away from Heston on October 9th, had a flight with no delays, and he nearly caught up Hill, who had nearly caught up Matthews. On October 18th, as Matthews crossed the Timor Sea, none of the three knew where the others were. At Darwin, lookouts with binoculars waited to see which would arrive first. It was Matthews. After landing, he asked the crowd 'Where's Hill?' They repeated 'Where's Hill?' and he knew he had won. Hill (like Hinkler and Kingsford-Smith a Queenslander) had, in fact, crashed at Atamboea, attempting to take-off for Darwin. He did not arrive until December 10th. Smithy got to Darwin the day after Matthews, setting a new time of nine days, twenty-one hours, forty minutes. Matthews had taken thirty-two days. He returned to England by ship, but his Puss Moth stayed in Australia, to become VH-UQB. •

64

64. F.R. Matthews' Puss Moth at Croydon before the flight, 16th September 1930.

TELEPHONES: B4330. B5952
CABLES AND TELEGRAMS: "AIRWAYS." PERTH

AIR MAIL ROUTES:
PERTH TO WYNDHAM. W.A.
PERTH TO ADELAIDE. S.A.

BOX M932. G.P.O., PERTH

35 A.M.P. CHAMBERS. PERTH. W.A.

October 16, 1930.

Messrs. A. D. C. Aircraft Ltd.,
Regent House,
Kingsway,
London, W.C.2. Eng.

HOURS FLOWN BY PUMA AND NIMBUS ENGINES

IN SERVICE OF

WEST AUSTRALIAN AIRWAYS LIMITED

The total mileage flown by the Puma and Nimbus-engined aircraft operated by West Australian Airways Limited now exceeds 1,400,000 miles. Of this mileage the Nimbus-engined aircraft have covered over 400,000 miles.

The successful record of this Company has been made possible by the reliability of these engines.

WEST AUSTRALIAN AIRWAYS LIMITED

N. Brearley.

Managing Director.

A TESTIMONY TO CROYDON-BUILT AERO ENGINES IN SERVICE WITH AN AUSTRALIAN AIRLINE, 1930

As this letter testifies, Nimbus engines built by the Aircraft Disposal Company at Croydon had, by October 1930, flown in excess of 400,000 miles. West Australian Airways was formed by Major Norman Brearley, whose signature appears on the letter, in August 1921. It started its services in December, flying north from Perth, with a Bristol Tourer, G-AUDI, which unfortunately crashed on the inaugural flight. This was one of six bought by W.A.A. Later they flew D.H.50s (from 1927) and D.H.60s (from 1928). One of their D.H.60s was Cobham's famous G-EBFO (see p4). In 1929 they bought four D.H.66 triple-engined biplanes for a service across the vast barren Nullarbor Plain, eastward from Perth to Adelaide. Some D.H.50s were equipped with 300hp A.D.C. Nimbus engines. D.H.60 Moths were powered by a variety of engines, most of them built by A.D.C., from the 60hp Cirrus I to the 105hp Cirrus Hermes I.

West Australian Airways was the airline joined by Charles Kingsford-Smith in 1921; he test-flew their first Bristol Tourer. W.A.A. was bought up by Adelaide Airways in 1936. •

66. *Oscar Garden sets off. The wrapped object is a spare air-screw.*

OSCAR GARDEN'S FLIGHT TO AUSTRALIA, 1930

Oscar Garden just missed taking part in the Matthews/Hill/Kingsford-Smith 'race'. He was a Scot, aged twenty-seven, from Sutherland, who had been in Australia and New Zealand for eleven years. In 1930 he came back to Britain on holiday and became enamoured of aviation. He took flying lessons at Norwich, and, after twenty hours flying experience, decided he would fly back to Australasia. He bought (apparently from Selfridges!) a Gipsy Moth which had belonged to Gordon Selfridge Junior, G-AASA, giving up his car in part exchange. He named it *Kia Ora*, Maori for 'good luck'. When he left Croydon Airport in it, on September 16th, he still had had only some forty hours in the air. He headed for Lympne, near the coast in Sussex, but this was covered in cloud, and he had to land elsewhere to ask the way. Finally arriving at Lympne, he waited until the next day for his take-off from England.

Despite his inexperience he met with only relatively minor set-backs on the way. He broke no records, but arrived in Australia in eleven days, just one more than Hinkler had taken. His landing, on November 4th, was at Wyndham, south-west of Darwin. He was the first airman from England to use this as an initial landing-place. On the way he had met, at Jask in Iran, Mildred, the Hon. Mrs. Victor Bruce, a long-distance flier and a lady well-known at Croydon Airport, where she ran several companies. She was engaged on a world tour in her Blackburn Bluebird IV, G-ABDS, *Bluebird*, and they flew to Karachi together. Garden flew on to Jhansi, on his own, where his first really bad landing occurred, and he overturned his aircraft. There was not much damage, but some delay, and at Calcutta he met Mrs. Bruce again. They then flew Calcutta-Akyab-Rangoon together, where they parted, she going off to Tokio.

In Australia, Garden shipped *Kia Ora* to New Zealand, where his relatives were, and gained there a commercial pilot's licence. At the end of his flying career, in the 1940s, he was chief pilot of Tasman Empire Airways Ltd. •

67. *Oscar Garden and* Kia Ora *in New Zealand in 1931.*

THE BRITISH-AUSTRALIAN EXPERIMENTAL AIR MAIL, FROM CROYDON, 1931

The England to India scheduled air service was begun by Imperial Airways in 1929. They then considered extending this, in conjunction with the Australian authorities, to link with Australia. It was decided that, as an experiment, two air mail deliveries should take place in each direction in April and May 1931. The first service from London — Croydon Airport — was to leave on April 4th. Which aircraft took it on the first stage does not seem to be recorded; but it was one of Imperial Airways' fleet of triple-engined Armstrong Whitworth Argosies, and the mail flew on the normal scheduled service as far as Delhi. Here, a de Havilland D.H.66 Hercules G-EBMW, *City of Cairo,* was to take it on to Darwin. However, *City of Cairo* crashed at Koepang, on the island of Timor, on April 19th. Imperial Airways then chartered *Southern Cross* from A.N.A. to fly the Timor Sea and rescue the mail. Charles Kingsford-Smith himself flew over and carried the mail to Darwin, six days late. Q.A.N.T.A.S. then carried the mail on to Brisbane, and then A.N.A. again, with the Avro Ten VH-UNA, *Southern Sun*, took it to Sydney, from where VH-UMG, *Southern Star*, flew it on to Melbourne. The return mail was flown by *Southern Star* to Sydney on 23rd April. (The pilot was Captain Patrick Windsor Lynch-Blosse, Welsh born, who went to Australia and took up flying in the 1920s. He later returned to Britain and became chief pilot of Spartan Air Lines, and made a charter flight from Lympne to Wyndham, then around Australia and back to England, between October 10 and December 26, 1933, in a ▶

FIRST [illegible]R MAIL TO AUSTRALIA.

11,000 MILES IN 15 DAYS.

LONDON TO PORT DARWIN.

From HARRY HARPER, Author of "The Romance of a Modern Airway."

ANOTHER landmark is to be reached in aerial history.

As a result of an agreement announced officially last night between the Air Ministry, the Post Office, and Imperial Airways, two demonstration air mail services are to be flown between England and Australia.

The distance of 11,194 miles between London and Port Darwin, Australia, will be covered in 15 days, as compared with 28 days by the fastest surface transport.

The idea is to show the practicability of an air mail across the Empire. Proposals for a regular weekly England-Australia service have been drawn up by Imperial Airways and are before the Governments concerned.

The first demonstration flight to Australia is to leave the London air station on Saturday. The machine, a big Armstrong Siddeley Argosy, will carry the first Australian mail and the weekly Indian and Central African air mails.

68

68. Cutting from the Daily Mail, *March 31st, 1931. The news item goes on to call Cairo 'now the "aerial Clapham Junction" of the East' and to say that when the weekly service is in existence 'the entire flight from London to Darwin will be accomplished regularly in 10 to 12 days'.*

Notice for Post Office Daily List 21st April 1931.

England-India Air Service - Experimental extension to Australia.

The Indian Air Mail due to leave London on Saturday, April 25, will be extended experimentally from Delhi to Port Darwin, Australia. Correspondence for the Straits Settlements and Malay States, Australia and New Zealand will be despatched by this service. The inclusive (postage and air) charges will be 1s. per half-ounce to the Straits Settlements and the Malay States, and 1s.4d. per half-ounce to Australia and New Zealand (by ordinary route from Australia).

The times of transmission are expected to be

to Singapore 13 days
to Port Darwin 16 days.
to Sydney 19 days

The latest times of posting will be the same as for the Indian Service, that is, 6 a.m. on Saturday morning in the Air Mail posting box at the G.P.O.London, and correspondingly earlier elsewhere.

M.

20 April 1931.

69

69. From the Post Office archives: the announcement of the experimental service for the Post Office Daily List of 21st April 1931.

70. A D.H. 66 Hercules; a sister-aircraft of City of Cairo, *whose crash marred the first experimental service.*

70

AUSTRALIAN AIR MAIL

CRASH ON TIMOR ISLAND

FROM OUR CORRESPONDENT

SYDNEY, APRIL 19

The Imperial Airways liner City of Cairo, carrying the first Australian air mail, crashed at Kupang, Timor, this afternoon. The occupants are unhurt and

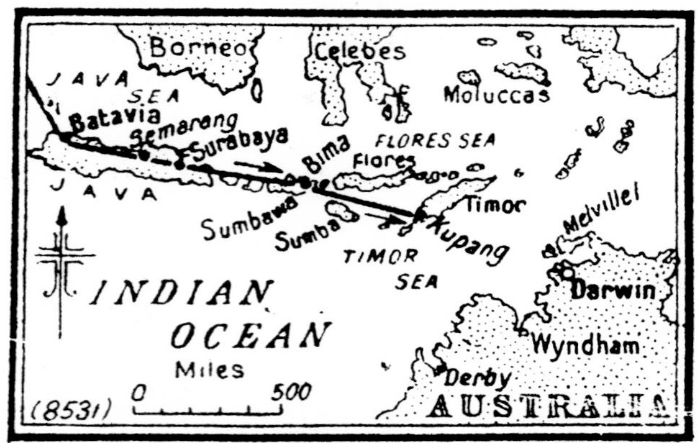

the mails safe, but the machine is too badly damaged to be repaired at Kupang.

BRISBANE, April 19.—Following the crash of the City of Cairo at Kupang arrangements are being made to convey the mails to Australia by an Australian aeroplane.—*Reuter.*

71

Spartan Cruiser.) The 1931 mail went Sydney-Brisbane by *Southern Sun*; then by Q.A.N.T.A.S. in the D.H.61 Giant Moth VH-UJB *Apollo*. Kingsford-Smith then took it in *Southern Cross* to Akyab, where Imperial Airways took over with the Hercules G-AARY *City of Karachi*. The mail reached Croydon on May 14th, as originally scheduled.

The second service again began from Croydon, on the scheduled India service of Imperial Airways. *City of Karachi* took it on to Akyab. Here, *Southern Cross* again, with Smithy and G.U. 'Scotty' Allan, flew it on to Darwin, arriving there one day late, on 11th May. Then Q.A.N.T.A.S. flew it to Brisbane in the D.H.50 VH-ULG *Hippomenes*. A.N.A. then took over again, with Avro Ten VH-UMI *Southern Moon*, and, from Sydney, another Ten, VH-UMH, *Southern Sky*.

For the return flight, A.N.A. brought mail from Melbourne to Brisbane in *Southern Sun* (flown by Jim Mollison), and Q.A.N.T.A.S. took it to Darwin in *Hippomenes*, flown by W. Hudson Fysh, managing director. From here, Imperial Airways took it all the way to Britain. They had bought from West Australian Airways a D.H.66, VH-UJQ, later G-ABMT, *City of Cape Town*. This had been flown from Perth to Darwin. It took the mail to Karachi, piloted by Captain R.P. Mollard (the pilot who crashed in *City of Cairo*, for which this Hercules was a replacement), from where it was picked-up on the regular service, reaching Croydon on June 4th, although scheduled for May 27th.

Apart from the early disaster with *City of Cairo*, and the final delay, the experiment had been a success, and the viability of the link had been demonstrated. It was to be another three and a half years before a regular weekly service began, but it marked the beginning of the struggle at the Australia end, especially between Q.A.N.T.A.S. and A.N.A., for the contract when the time came. •

71. Left: Cutting from The Times *of 20th April 1931: the crash on Timor island. No cause for the accident is offered in the report from 'Our Aeronautical Correspondent' which follows, except that 'the pilot, Mr R.P. Mollard, complained of the intense heat when he arrived at Rangoon on Wednesday evening'.*

72. Opposite: From the Post Office archives: the timetable for the flights, with actual variations marked in.

TIME TABLE OF TWO EXPERIMENTAL FLIGHTS TO AUSTRALIA AND BACK.

OUTWARDS.

		I.	II.
London	Dep.	4th April	25th April
Delhi	(arr.	"	May
	(dep.	13th "	4th "
Allahabad	dep.	14th "	5th "
Akyab	dep.	15th "	6th "
Rangoon			
Victoria Point	dep.	16th "	7th "
Singapore	dep.	17th "	8th "
Sourabaya	dep.	18th "	9th "
Koepang	dep.	19th "	10th "
Darwin	arr.	19th "	10th "
	Actually arrived	21 April	11 May

HOMEWARDS.

		I.	II.
Darwin	dep.	27th April	17th May
Koepang	dep.	28th "	18th "
Sourabaya	dep.	29th "	19th "
Singapore	dep.	30th "	20th "
Victoria Point	dep.	1st May	21st "
Rangoon			
Akyab	dep.	2nd "	22nd "
Allahabad	dep.	3rd "	23rd "
Delhi	(arr.	3rd "	23rd "
	(dep.	5th "	25th "
London	arr.	14th "	31st "
	Actually arrived	14 May	4 June

The places mentioned between Delhi and Darwin are night stopping places.

72

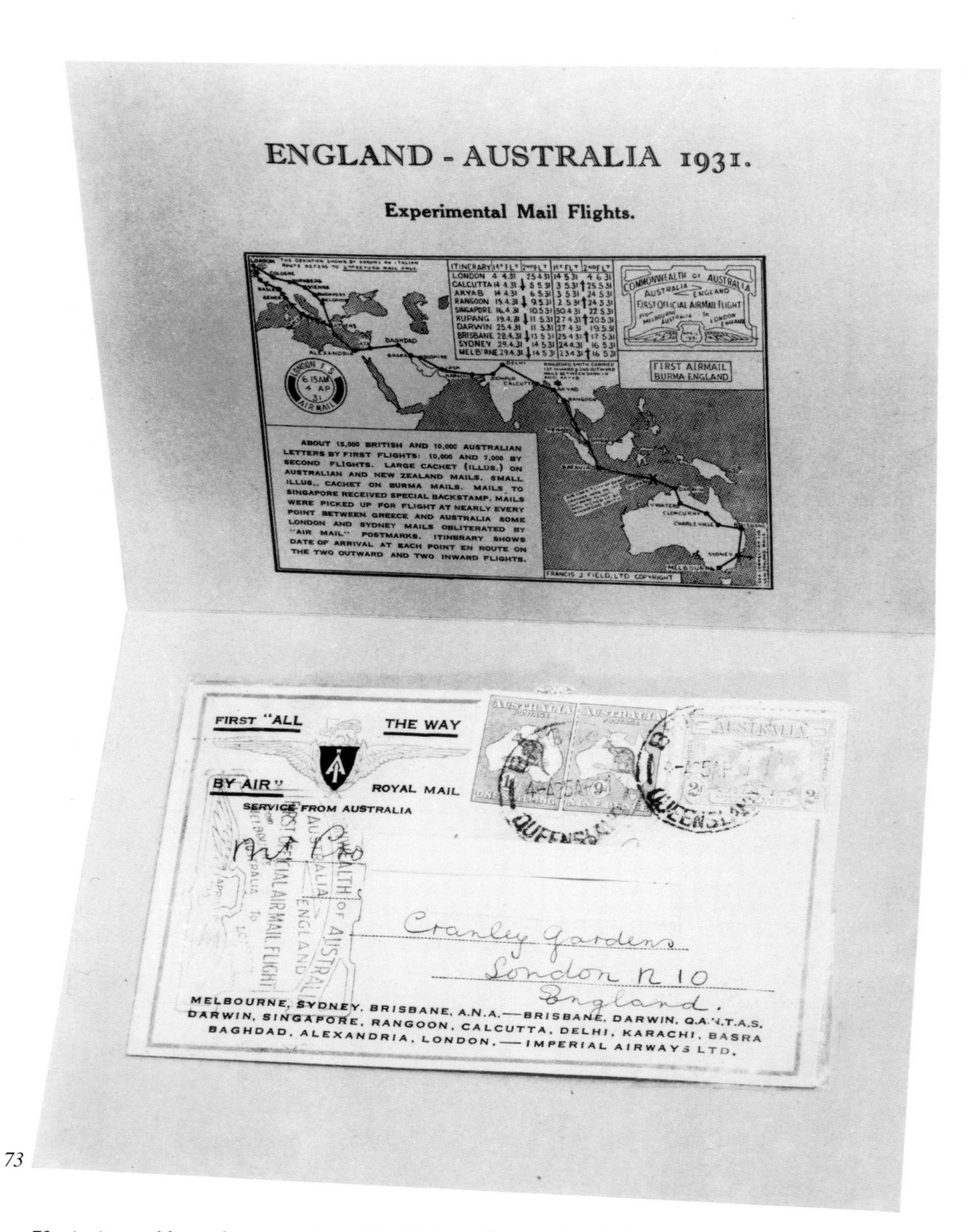

73

73. *An item addressed to a member of the* Flight *staff, carried in the first Australia-England air mail.*

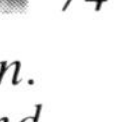

74. *The Gipsy Moth, VH-UFT, lands at Croydon. The aircraft was later re-registered as G-ABUB and toured with Cobham's National Aviation Day Displays Ltd.*

75. *Mollison and the kangaroo.*

JIM MOLLISON FLIES HOME FROM AUSTRALIA — TO CROYDON — IN UNDER NINE DAYS IN 1931

James Allan Mollison was born in Glasgow on April 19th 1905. In 1923 he took up flying and got a commission in the R.A.F., for which he was at one time a boxing champion. After a spell in India, he qualified as an instructor at the Central Flying School, and on leaving the R.A.F. in 1928, went to Australia and became an instructor for the Australian Aero Club; then flying for Eyre Peninsular Airways (1929–30) before, in 1930, becoming a pilot for Kingsford-Smith and Ulm's Australian National Airways. In 1931, just before A.N.A. ceased operating (see p 25), Mollison (who had flown no less than 1,200 hours for them by then) decided to fly home to Britain, and break the existing record on the way, held at that time by Charles W.A. Scott, who had taken it from Kingsford-Smith with a flight taking ten days, thirteen hours, twenty-five minutes, in May–June that year, flying a Gipsy Moth, VH-UQA.

A meeting with Scott, whom Jim had known in R.A.F. days, made him determined to become a celebrity long-distance flier too. Scott, too, introduced him to Lord Wakefield's manager in Australia, Cyril Westcott. Mollison managed to get Wakefield's backing for his flight, to the extent of having a special Gipsy Moth with steel fuel tanks built ▶

76

76. Two veterans of the England–Australia, Australia–England routes: Jim Mollison, with Amy Johnson, to whom he was now married, standing at Croydon by their D.H. Dragon, G-ACCV, Seafarer. *In this they tried to take-off on the morning of June 8th 1933 in an attempt on the world's long-distance record, which was to begin with a trans-Atlantic flight. The undercarriage of the aircraft collapsed on take-off under the heavily-laden machine. They later got away from Pendine Sands in Wales, and made the Atlantic crossing, but crashed short of New York on the other side.*

for him. The steel tanks probably saved his life when he hit a telegraph pole attempting to leave Darwin on June 7th, as they did not burst, spraying petrol on a hot engine, as he believed would have been the case with aluminium ones. Lord Wakefield rebuilt the aircraft for him, and he took off again, this time from Wyndham, on July 29th.

As Mollison later wrote: 'When Cyril waved me off again on my second and last chance to make good I'd burned all my boats. My job I'd resigned again, my clothes were either sold or given away, in my pocket was £5, all the money I had. It had to do for spending-money on the way to England . . . I got to England roughly a day and a half inside Scott's time. I had £4 left of my £5. The odd £1 had gone on liquor. I had been accommodated at night by men and women of the Empire who would not see a British pilot flying to pseudo glory go hungry and uncared for to bed.' In fact, Jim had done the trip in eight days, nineteen hours and twenty-five minutes. As told in *The First, the Fastest and the Famous*, he was certainly in poor shape when he arrived at Croydon on August 6th. He was ultra-tired; his eyes were suffering the effects of his having lost his goggles over India, and there was fog over the aerodrome which caused him to overshoot. Mollison's own words are: '. . . I was now bored and very tired of flying by myself. I felt suddenly glad when I saw Croydon. Then the crowd dawned on my consciousness. People perched on roofs and overflowed the aerodrome. There were red carpets out, platforms, masses of important-looking cars in ordered rows. "Somebody important coming in, I s'pose", I surmised, and peered all round the sky for his aeroplane . . . Then comprehension dawned on me. It was I, the unknown, the honest burghers of the great Metropolis stood so patiently awaiting. I realised it and my eyes swam a bit when I landed. I was awfully tired and sleepy.' Some bright publicity man had brought on a boxing kangaroo to greet him. It tried to hit him with a left hook to the jaw, and, in Mollison's words: 'kicked me violently in the stomach' — probably just what he needed at this time.

However, Jim was taken that night to Grosvenor House, given the use of a suite of rooms free, and entertained at a banquet. Next day he woke up an instant celebrity. He became the 'Playboy of the Air' as the title of his iconoclastic 1937 autobiography proclaimed. He married Amy Johnson. Never a saint, Jim Mollison also perhaps never really suffered from self-delusions, and did not lack a sense of the ridiculous. His achievements were real. His later solo record-breaking flights included England–Cape Town, March 1932; North Atlantic, first westward solo, August 1932; first England–South America flight and first westward solo South Atlantic, Februrary 1933; and, with Edouard Corniglion-Molinier, first flight New York–London (Croydon). Jim married twice more after his divorce from Amy; his second marriage also ending in divorce. He died in October 1959. •

77. Lt.Cdr. Hall with his Bluebird IV at Croydon before the Australia flight. 77

LT.CDR. HALL FLIES A BLUEBIRD TO AUSTRALIA FROM CROYDON, 1932

A different machine to fly to Australia in 1932 was a Blackburn Bluebird IV, G-AAVG, with a 115hp Hermes II engine. The pilot was Lt. Commander Geoffrey Aitken Hall, a serving naval officer, thirty-one years old. The aircraft had been one of the fourteen Bluebird IVs entered for the 1930 King's Cup Air Race (then flown by Sqn.Ldr. L. Slatter).

Hall took off from Croydon on August 8th, 1932. His flight took twenty-four days, three of them spent in the search for two aviators, Salt and Taylor, who had disappeared between Singapore and Rangoon on a flight to England. Hall appears to have made no attempt to break records. He reached Wyndham on September 1st and then flew on towards Melbourne, via Perth (where his brother was on the staff of the military headquarters) and Adelaide. Between Adelaide and Melbourne occurred his only forced landing of the whole flight; appropriately enough at Hall's Gap in the Australian Grampians. He appears to have been helped on his way by the Vacuum Oil Company's aviation officer. The Bluebird remained in Australia, becoming VH-UQZ. Hall left the navy in 1938 and went to New Guinea, where he flew for W.R. Carpenter Airlines, operating between Sydney and New Guinea. He took part in World War II as an air liaison officer with the Royal Australian Navy, later performing other functions with the R.A.N. and R.A.A.F. He retired from the Royal Australian Navy in 1956. •

FIRST SOLO FLIGHT BY A WOMAN FROM AUSTRALIA TO ENGLAND, MADE BY AN AUSTRALIAN, REACHES CROYDON, JUNE 1933

I have been confused about the personal name of Mrs. Harry Barrington Bonney as opposed to that of her husband. The press at the time resolutely called her nothing but Mrs. Harry — or Harry B. — Bonney. For *The First, the Fastest and the Famous* I sought her forename, and gave it, from a source which appears to have been incorrect, as 'Violet'. She was, however, christened Maude Rose following her birth on November 20th, 1897 (her maiden name was Rubens) but for some reason has always been known as 'Lores'.

In August 1932, Lores Bonney, who had taken up flying some time before, announced plans for an attempt to fly solo round Australia, which no woman had yet done. Her aircraft was the Gipsy Moth G-ABEN, by this time VH-UPV, which Cedric Hill had flown from England in 1930 (see p. 39). Her flight, which was successful, began on August 15th 1932 from Archerfield Aerodrome, Brisbane, and finished there forty-two days later, on September 27th. She had had problems on the way, mainly with bad landings and weather, but she had made it.

78

78. Lores Bonney: a photograph taken when she had just made her round-Australia flight.

In April 1933, at a time when Bert Hinkler's body was still waiting to be found on an Italian mountain, Lores Bonney set out to be the first woman to fly from Australia to England. It was April 10th, and among the people to see her off at Archerfield were members of the Hinkler family. Lores was related by marriage to Bert Hinkler, whose mother, Frances Bonney, was Harry Bonney's cousin. From Archerfield, Brisbane, she made her across Australia to Darwin, which she reached on April 13th. This was the day after Bill Lancaster had crashed *Southern Cross Minor* in the Tanezrouft.

She took off on April 15th, but after a few days her aircraft came to grief in a crash-landing on an island called Bang Biang near Siam (Thailand), and she was reported missing for a few days. The Gipsy Moth had to be extensively repaired, which took about a month, before she was able to leave Calcutta, to which the aircraft had been shipped, on 20th May. On June 21st, seventy-three days after leaving Brisbane, and sixty-eight from Darwin, Lores Bonney reached Croydon. Few people met her, partly because there was some confusion over whether she intended to land at Croydon or Heston (north of London).

Charles Grey wrote in *The Aeroplane* on July 12th 1933: 'In conversation after dinner Mrs. Bonney said that she had arrived at Croydon the previous week-end without advising anybody in this country of her impending arrival except the airport officials at Croydon. The result was that she was, quite naturally, treated as any other incoming aircraft, and there was nobody to receive her. When she got to London she found that all the people to whom she had letters of introduction had gone away for the week-end and consequently she spent her first week-end in England entirely alone without a soul to speak to, — which is about the grimmest experience which any visitor to this country can have.

Actually, Mr. Harold Perrin of the Royal Aero Club was hunting about London for two or three days trying to find out where Mrs. Bonney was staying, because he had a mass of mail waiting for her at the Royal Aero Club . . . Mrs. Bonney is not a publicity hunter, so probably she doesn't mind the lack of publicity, but certainly all we people in aviation regret that she was not properly received.' The following week he apologised, because, ' . . . When she landed at Croydon she was actually welcomed by a "crowd" consisting of the representative of the Wakefield company and two photographers who happened to be at Croydon and joined in the "stampede" towards the machine.

79

79. Lores Bonney airborne in her Gipsy Moth VH-UPV, in which she became the first woman to fly round Australia, and the first woman to fly solo from Australia to Britain.

Shortly after she landed Mr. L.H. Pike, the Acting Agent-General for Queensland, whence Mrs. Bonney hails, arrived at Croydon post-haste, or as soon as he could possibly have got there after hearing that she was expected.

Such a welcome was meagre enough, but as Mrs. Bonney only advised Croydon of her impending arrival, all the more credit is due to those who were present to receive her.'

Lores Bonney was later the first woman to fly from Australia to South Africa, in 1933, and in 1934 she was given the M.B.E. ●

80

80. Astraea *at Croydon before the flight with, from left to right, Mr. Griffiths, Flight Engineer; Major Brackley; the Croydon representative of the Marconi company (up-to-date radio and navigational equipment was carried, but this did not prevent the aircraft getting lost over Queensland); Captain Prendergast; W.E. Hickman, representative of Armstrong Whitworth. It is he who signed the picture before giving it to the late Jack Crowson, of Imperial Airways and later B.O.A.C., who lodged in the same house as he in Wallington.*

IMPERIAL AIRWAYS SURVEY FLIGHT FOR NEW 'EMPIRE AIR ROUTE' SERVICE TO AUSTRALIA — FROM CROYDON, 1933

Following the experimental air mail, and Kingsford-Smith's all-Australian air mail, the next move towards establishing a regular passenger and air mail service between Britain and Australia was the survey flight of 1933. On May 29th the Armstrong Whitworth A.W.15 Atalanta, G-ABTL, *Astraea* left Croydon Airport to fly to Melbourne to test a route, and then return to Karachi where it was to be employed on the India service. The Atalantas were Imperial Airways' first monoplanes, and their first four-engined aircraft; especially designed for the tropical sections of their routes. The pilot for the survey flight was a Captain Prendergast, apparently Archer Robert Prendergast, although several sources which I have previously followed give his initials as 'J.V.'. The flight was under the command of the Air Superintendent of Imperial Airways, Herbert George Brackley, usually known as Major Brackley, or Brackles (later Air Commodore Brackley). *Astraea* failed to meet her schedule by seven days, part of the delay being caused by a fuel shortage on the last (Timor Sea) leg of the flight, when she had to land on Bathurst Island and await supplies by boat from the mainland. Darwin was reached on June 18th. From there, the flight continued to Melbourne, where they arrived on June 29th. *Astraea* was the first four-engined aeroplane to fly in Australia. They went via towns which included Brisbane, headquarters of Q.A.N.T.A.S., where speeches at a celebration dinner were on the theme of future co-operation.

Whilst *Astraea* was making her way across Australia, Charles Ulm and other survivors of A.N.A. were setting off for London in the Avro Ten VH-UXX, formerly VH-UMI, *Southern Moon*, now renamed *Faith in Australia*. Their aim was to gain publicity to get backing so that they could submit a tender for the Australian end of the new service (tenders had to be in before January 1934). They reached Heston after seventeen days, badly delayed by engine trouble in India and in France.

As *Astraea* made her way back across Australia, Hudson Fysh, managing director of Q.A.N.T.A.S., joined them at Longreach, Queensland, to do his own survey of the route to England. Leaving Australia they encountered monsoon rains. At Akyab they met Jim Woods, from Perth but born in Aberdeen, a pilot for West Australian Airways, who was attempting a flight to England in a Gipsy Moth, VH-UPD, *Spirit of Western Australia*. This Moth had a streamlined canopy, making the cockpit into a tiny cabin. He, too, had problems with the monsoons, to which he was much more vulnerable than the Atalanta, and by which he was held up. However, by August 17th he had made it to Rome, from where he flew non-stop to Croydon, forty-two days after leaving Broome in Australia. By this time, Brackley and Fysh had been in London for about a month, arriving back at Croydon on board the Handley Page H.P.42 G-AAGX *Hannibal*. *Astraea* had remained at Karachi, and Prendergast with it. In September Imperial Airways extended regular services to Rangoon, and they would link with Australia shortly. •

81

Imperial Airways "Astraea," arriving at Mascot Aerodrome, Sydney, after concluding the survey by Major Brackley of the final sections of the England-Australia air route. The next section will be opened in September.

81. Illustration and caption from Air and Airways *magazine, September 1933.*

82

A MONOSPAR THAT WENT TO AUSTRALIA FROM CROYDON — AND ONE THAT TRIED BUT FAILED

General Aircraft Ltd., formed at Croydon Aerodrome in 1931/32, grew out of the Monospar Wing Co. Ltd., a company started a year or so earlier to exploit the design of the Swiss-born engineer, W.J.Steiger. He invented the 'Monospar' form of construction, building a very strong monoplane wing around a single duralumin girder spar with a pyramidal system of tie-rods for bracing, which was then fabric-covered. The first whole aeroplane built to this design was designated ST-3 (STs -1 and -2 had been wings only) and was constructed by the Gloster Aircraft Co., but the rest were built by G.A.L., at first in the old Aircraft Disposal Company hangars at Croydon, until G.A.L. moved to larger premises at Hanworth, Middlesex. At Croydon, the ST-4s (two marks) and ST-6s were constructed. One of the ST-4 Mk.IIs was G-ACHS (*below*) which left Croydon on October 23rd 1933, on an attempted flight to Australia. The pilot was Henry ('Jerry') Shaw, and he was accompanied by G.A. Guillermin as engineer. The aircraft belonged to the Asiatic Petroleum Co., for which Jerry Shaw worked. This evidently was, or was part of, Shell-Mex, as the purpose of the flight appears to have been to inspect the Shell organisation at aerodromes along the route. He expected to reach Melbourne on December 27th. However, a crash probably somewhere in what is now Iraq or Iran (there are conflicting accounts) ended the flight on November 10th, and the aircraft was shipped home. Jerry Shaw had the distinction of piloting the first recognised commercial flight across the Channel on July 15th, 1919, later flying for K.L.M., but is best remembered as Shell-Mex representative at Croydon.

Above is one of the only two Monospar ST-11s built (at Hanworth), both for Australia; VH-UAZ and VH-USN. The aircraft, seen here at Croydon before delivery, probably in September 1934, is believed to be VH-UAZ, ordered, apparently, by the Australian Department of Civil Aviation. The ST-11 was a variant of the ST-10, its only significant difference, apart from extra equipment, being its retractable undercarriage. ●

83

84

84. VH-USC at Croydon before the first Q.E.A. delivery flight. With the Croydon control tower behind them are, left to right: Capt. Lester Brain, Dick Price and Reg Pink. The co-pilot and engineer were seconded from Imperial Airways.

QANTAS EMPIRE AIRWAYS IS FORMED — AND RECEIVES ITS FIRST AIRCRAFT VIA CROYDON, 1934

Q.A.N.T.A.S. stood for Queensland and Northern Territory Aerial Services Ltd., i.e. it was originally an internal regional service. It had been formed in 1919 by Paul McGinnis and Hudson Fysh. Along with Kingsford-Smith and Ulm's Australian National Airways it had taken part in the 1931 experimental England-Australia, Australia-England air mail, and then battled with A.N.A. for the mail contract at the Australian end, which it was to win. First, however, in January 1934, a new company for external flights, QANTAS Empire Airways, was formed in co-operation between Q.A.N.T.A.S. and Imperial Airways, each holding fifty per cent of the capital. In April the new company was awarded the government air mail contract between Australia and Singapore. Up to now, Q.A.N.T.A.S. had used single-engined aircraft. To gain this contract it had had to agree to operate the service with a new type of multi-engined aircraft being produced by de Havilland to a specification issued by the Australian government in 1933 for a high-performance mail and passenger aeroplane. This, designed and built in four months, was the D.H.86. The prototype bore a strong family resemblance to the D.H.84 Dragon, which preceded it, and the production aircraft to the D.H.89 Dragon Rapide, which followed hot on their heels. Both of these were twin-engined aircraft, though, whilst the D.H.86 (never officially named but often referred to as the de Havilland ▶

85

85. A full profile view of VH-USC (later named Canberra*) with a Handley Page H.P.42 of Imperial Airways between it and the control tower, whose distinctive radio mast towers above it; and, left background, the old A.D.C. hangars, by now housing other aircraft firms.*

86

86. VH-USC in flight near Hatfield Aerodrome, Herts., where it was built.

'Express' or 'Air Express') was powered by four de Havilland Gipsy Six engines. Ten passengers could be carried.

All Q.A.N.T.A.S. pilots would have to go on a conversion course. Lester Brain, at this time their chief pilot, was sent to England to test-fly the D.H.86 and fly back to Australia in one. He duly left from Croydon on 24th September 1934 in the first Q.E.A. D.H.86, registered VH-USC (the first of six ordered for the airline). With him as crew went R.U. (Dick) Price, First Officer, and R.A. (Reg) Pink, Flight Engineer. They arrived at Darwin on 10th October and Brisbane (Archerfield) on 13th October.

Then came alarm. Another airline, Holyman's, flying from Tasmania to Melbourne, had already purchased the first production D.H.86, VH-URN, *Miss Hobart*, which had been shipped out to Australia. On October 19th this suddenly plunged into the sea and was lost without trace, for no apparent cause, resulting in the deaths of Victor Holyman himself, who was flying it, and his co-pilot and ten passengers. Soon after, Q.E.A.'s second D.H.86 delivery flight began, when Archer Prendergast, who had flown *Astraea* (p50), left Croydon in VH-USG, with W.V. Creetes and F.R. Charlton as crew. They reached Darwin on 13th November, but then crashed on 15th November near Longreach, with no survivors. Naturally, an Air Investigation Committee was set up, and tests made on the D.H.86s, which were grounded. No single major problem was identified, but the tail fin was strengthened and the load distribution adjusted. After this unfortunate start the D.H.86 gave good service, not only to Q.E.A., but to other airlines, including Imperial Airways and Railway Air Services at Croydon.

After World War II there was still QANTAS Empire Airways and Q.A.N.T.A.S. (or QANTAS). B.O.A.C., successor to Imperial Airways, still owned half of Q.E.A. At the end of 1946 the Australian government enabled QANTAS to buy out B.O.A.C., and then in June 1947 themselves bought QANTAS, which henceforth became the state-owned flag carrier. ●

87

87. Hengist *with Air Mail Pennant and Civil Air Ensign before the flight.*

'A DREAM COME TRUE': FIRST REGULAR WEEKLY AIR MAIL SERVICE TO AUSTRALIA STARTS FROM CROYDON, DECEMBER 1934

On Saturday 8th December 1934, around lunchtime, a special ceremony was held in one of Imperial Airways' hangars at Croydon. The Handley Page H.P.42 airliner, G-AAXE, *Hengist*, was about to leave on the first leg of the first regular scheduled service for air mail to Australia. The long-planned-for link was about to be forged.

1934 had seen other flights 'down under' besides the Q.E.A. delivery flights. In September Freda Thompson, at twenty-two years of age, began the first England to Australia solo flight by an Australian woman, leaving Lympne on the 28th and arriving at Darwin on November 10th, in a Gipsy Moth Major, G-ACUC. Oddly enough, Lord Sempill, a former chairman and then president of the Royal Aeronautical Society, left the same place on the same day on a flight which was intended originally only to take him to various places in western Europe where he had aviation business. However, having also interests in places further afield, including Australia, where among other things he wished to be present at Melbourne's Centenary celebrations, he flew on, and arrived at Darwin on 21st November. His aircraft was a D.H. Puss Moth, G-ABJU. This was the first 'casual' flight to Australia.

Also in 1934 there had been flown the most important air race of the 1930s: the Mildenhall to Melbourne 'MacRobertson' race, for which the de Havilland Company designed and built the famous D.H.88 Comets, three of which took part in this epic race. This was won by Charles Scott and Tom Campbell Black in the D.H.88 G-ACSS, *Grosvenor House*, reducing the time to Australia to two days, four and a half hours and just under seventy-one hours from Mildenhall, Suffolk to Melbourne (see p62).

It was against this background that *Hengist* sat in the hangar on December 8th with a dais beneath its wings, on which was a bevy of VIPs. They included Lord Londonderry, Secretary of State for Air, who handed letters from the King (George V), the Queen, the Prince of Wales (the future Edward VIII), and others, to Sir Kingsley Wood, the Postmaster General, to despatch. The theme of Lord Londonderry's speech was the 'cordial collaboration of the Governments of India and the Dominion and Colonial Governments concerned which had made possible the through service'. Sir Kingsley Wood received the letters, 'thumped them with his rubber stamp' (*The Aeroplane*), and said that when the first service from Croydon to Karachi was sent off five and half years ago, there were 8,000 letters. Now there were 100,000 letters and 500lbs. of parcels — about two tons in all. The Rt. Hon. S.M. Bruce, Australian ▶

88

89. *The 'typical London postman', the blue air mail bag, and the stamp with which the letters 'had just been thumped'.*

88. *Left to right (foreground): a postman; Sir Kingsley Wood (Postmaster-General); and Lord Londonderry, Secretary of State for Air. Of this part of the ceremony,* The Aeroplane *said, on December 12th 1934: 'Sir Kingsley Wood and a typical London postman then wrestled with a blue air mail bag and the special letters which had just been thumped. One very big letter would not go in the bag. The postman started to fold it, in the manner to which most of us are accustomed among the wreckage which comes through our letter-boxes, and strange cracking noises showed that the contents were suffering. The postman appealed to Sir Kingsley Wood. He shook his head. The bag was sealed and handed with the cracked letter to Sir Eric Geddes ...'*

89

High Commissioner, a former Australian Prime Minister (see p5), could not be present, but sent a message 'with a good Imperial ring about it'. Sir James Parr, New Zealand High Commissioner, said how important 'our Imperial Airways would be if another war started'. Sir Eric Geddes, Chairman of Imperial Airways, said it was 'as a dream come true' (but regretted that Canada and New Zealand were not yet included in the Imperial air mail system). Others present included Sir Philip Sassoon, Under Secretary of State for Air, and Mr. George Woods Humphery, Managing Director of Imperial Airways.

The pilot of *Hengist* was to be Leslie Allen Walters (who lived nearby in Foxley Lane, Purley). The tractors towed *Hengist* out of the hangar, proudly flying its Civil Air Ensign and the Air Mail Pennant.

Hengist took the mail as far as Karachi. It was being sent out east to fly the Cairo-Karachi route, and this constituted a positioning flight. It was destroyed in a hangar fire at Karachi in 1937, the only one of the eight H.P.42s to be lost before the war. From Karachi to Darwin, *Astraea* (see p50) took over, with the help of the Atalanta VT-AEF, *Arethusa*. They arrived on 18th December.

From Darwin on to Mt. Isa QANTAS Empire Airways took over, and the flight was made by the D.H.61 VH-UJC *Diana* flown by Scotty Allan, formerly of A.N.A., and the D.H.50J VH-ULG *Hippomenes* with Capt. Lester Brain. *Diana* was damaged at Camooweal, and its cargo transferred to *Hippomenes*. The last leg, Mt. Isa to Brisbane, was flown by the D.H.50A VH-UJS, piloted by Eric Donaldson. The new D.H.86s should have made these flights, but they were still grounded at this time after the early tragedies (see p53). The mail reached Brisbane on December 21st.

The first service in the other direction was inaugurated on December 10th by the Duke of Gloucester, at Archerfield, Brisbane. Lord Sempill was there too, having flown on by a route which included Alice Springs, Adelaide, Melbourne, Canberra and Sydney. He made a point of flying over Bert Hinkler's birthplace, ▶

Bundaberg, and when he landed at Rockhampton he sent a message to Hinkler's mother which included Christmas greetings. By the time he returned to England his Puss Moth had flown 50,000 miles. It was an entirely different achievement from Hinkler's, but to a considerable degree it, together with the first regular air mail flights, and the MacRobertson race, marked the beginning of the end of the pioneering period of the England-Australia routes, of which Hinkler's flight had been the 'end of the beginning'.

The Australia-England first regular service was flown from Brisbane to Darwin in *Diana* (Lester Brain) and *Hippomenes* (to Roma, Queensland, Russell Tapp; on to Darwin, Scotty Allan). From Darwin it left on board *Arethusa* (flown by Rex Taylor). On the last leg, to Croydon from Paris, the mail was on board the Argosy G-AAEJ, *City of Coventry*, and the Short L.17, G-ACJK, *Syrinx*.

The Singapore-Brisbane (and return) sections of the first scheduled flights were for air mail only. The whole route was not opened for passengers for several months; until April 13th 1935 from Croydon to Brisbane, and from 17th April for Brisbane to Croydon. Because of heavy section bookings, no through passengers were carried on the 13th April flight. The first two passengers to fly all the way from Croydon to Brisbane were taken on the flight starting on April 20th. The single fare was £195, and the flight was scheduled to take twelve and a half days.

On May 6th 1936, the weekly service from Croydon was duplicated for the first time. From Brisbane, the twice-a-week service began ten days later.

In 1937, however, Imperial Airways' 'C' class flying-boats were introduced on the Australia and other Empire routes, and from March 5th took them over entirely, operating from their new Hythe base on Southampton Water. From this time, only the European services of Imperial Airways were flown from Croydon. It was the end of another era. ●

90. Hengist *on the apron with the Croydon control tower on the left.*

91. Hengist, *with engines running, prepares to leave.*

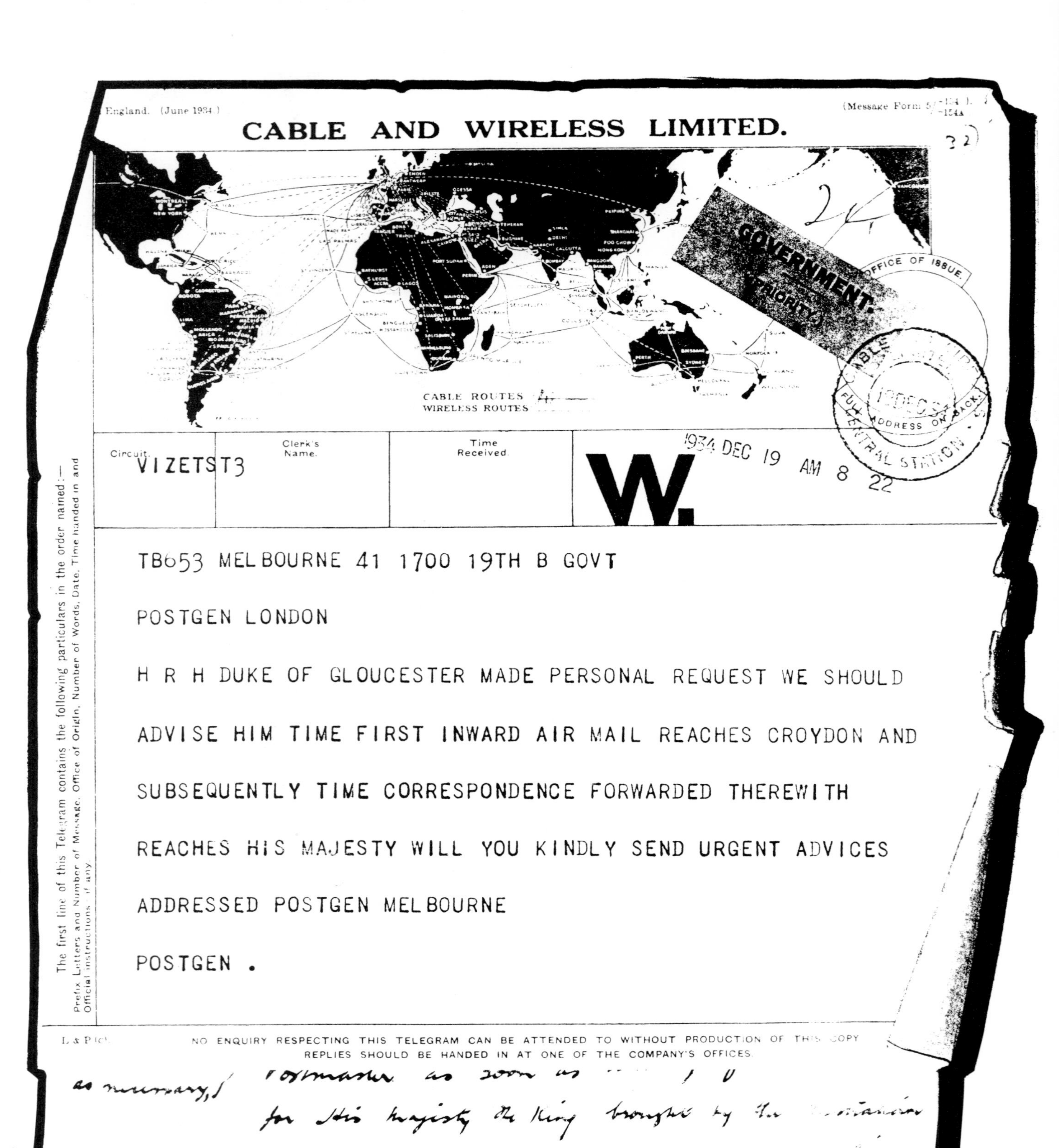
England. (June 1934.)

CABLE AND WIRELESS LIMITED.

CABLE ROUTES
WIRELESS ROUTES

The first line of this Telegram contains the following particulars in the order named:— Prefix Letters and Number of Message, Office of Origin, Number of Words, Date, Time handed in and Official instructions, if any.

Circuit.	Clerk's Name.	Time Received.	
VIZETST3			W. 1934 DEC 19 AM 8 22

TB653 MELBOURNE 41 1700 19TH B GOVT

POSTGEN LONDON

H R H DUKE OF GLOUCESTER MADE PERSONAL REQUEST WE SHOULD ADVISE HIM TIME FIRST INWARD AIR MAIL REACHES CROYDON AND SUBSEQUENTLY TIME CORRESPONDENCE FORWARDED THEREWITH REACHES HIS MAJESTY WILL YOU KINDLY SEND URGENT ADVICES ADDRESSED POSTGEN MELBOURNE

POSTGEN .

NO ENQUIRY RESPECTING THIS TELEGRAM CAN BE ATTENDED TO WITHOUT PRODUCTION OF THIS COPY
REPLIES SHOULD BE HANDED IN AT ONE OF THE COMPANY'S OFFICES.

92. *From the Post Office archives: a telegram from Melbourne on behalf of the Duke of Gloucester, who had seen the first Australia-England regular air mail service off, and wished to be informed when the mail reached Croydon, and when correspondence among it reached King George V (his brother).*

JEAN BATTEN — FIRST PERSON TO HOLD THE ENGLAND–AUSTRALIA RECORD IN BOTH DIRECTIONS, ON ARRIVAL AT CROYDON OCTOBER 1937

Jean Batten was born in Rotorua, New Zealand, in the heart of the district of geysers, springs, pools of boiling mud, and other thermal phenomena. The date was September 15th 1909; six weeks, as she herself was to write: 'after Blériot's historic flight across the English Channel' (Jean Batten, *My Life*). Also, it was some six years after the birth of Amy Johnson, with whom Jean was later often to be compared. Because almost everybody who came to New Zealand wanted to see the natural wonders of the thermal district, Rotorua was an international town of which 'a large part of the population was composed of tourists and my parents entertained an interesting variety of sportsmen and travelled people. It was therefore not surprising that even at the early age of two years I had developed a great desire to roam . . .'. The early flights to Australia, after the First World War, aroused much interest in New Zealand as well as Australia, and Jean was excited by them; but it was, she claimed, Bert Hinkler's flight and then Kingsford-Smith's trans-Pacific flight, that finally made her determined to become a pilot herself.

93

93 & 94. Jean Batten, 'New Zealand's famous air girl', in the cabin of her Percival Gull Six, G-ADPR, Jean, *from a contemporary cigarette card. Publication was evidently before her last great flight back to Croydon in October 1937.*

She was lucky enough to meet 'Smithy' when he was in New Zealand, and then, on a visit to Australia she met him again, and he offered her a flight. Up above the Blue Mountains, in *Southern Cross*, she knew she had found her true element. Her father, who himself was a dentist, wanted Jean to become a concert pianist (she was studying music in Auckland). Back home, she offered to sell her piano to pay for flying lessons, to her father's dismay. Her mother, however, was inclined to support her — the beginning of a rift which ended in divorce for Jean's parents. Helen Batten was going to visit England in 1929, and agreed to take her daughter with her. 'In England it seemed I should be in the centre of flying activity, and it would not be so difficult to make a start'. The piano was duly sold. In England, Helen Batten went along with nineteen-year-old Jean to the London Aeroplane Club, where Amy Johnson and other famous women pilot had learnt to fly, and helped her join and book her first flying lessons. Before they were due to return to New Zealand, Jean had gained her 'A' (private pilot's) licence. She did contemplate flying to Australia now, after only a few hours solo; but wiser counsels prevailed and she went back by sea with her mother; returning in 1931 to gain her 'B' or commercial pilot's licence. This involved, among other things, a night solo from Croydon to Lympne. She was having difficulty making ends meet on her allowance from home whilst having to spend thirty shillings an hour to hire an aeroplane. New Zealand was in the middle of a trade depression, and suddenly her income from her father stopped; but her mother helped, and she herself pawned some belongings. If she failed her night flight from Croydon, however, she would not be able to afford to try it again. Although she nearly did not make it when her instrument lights failed on the way back to Croydon, she did complete the flight with a torch which had been lent to her at Lympne, and got her licence. Next morning she flew victory spins over Croydon.

PHOTOCARDS
A Continuous Series of Topical Interest

JEAN BATTEN.

Miss Jean Batten, New Zealand's famous air girl, has accomplished many startling performances in recent years, and was the first woman to fly across the South Atlantic Ocean, a 2,000 miles "hop," taking her 18 hours 15 minutes. Flew to New Zealand in under eleven days, to create a record in 1936, receiving a wonderful reception on landing; and beat the solo flight record to Australia, on the way, by reaching the Antipodes in 5 days 21 hours 3 minutes. Miss Batten also holds the record for a flight from Lympne to Port Natal, Brazil, which she accomplished in 61¼ hours

Albums for Photocards on sale at Tobacconists Price 6d.
ARDATH TOBACCO CO: LTD: Manufacturers of
STATE EXPRESS AND ARDATH CIGARETTES
PACKED WITH KINGS THE LARGER CIGARETTES. 10 FOR 6d.

94

She was now determined to make a flight to Australia, and managed to find a backer, who agreed to help her buy a Moth against fifty per cent of anything made out of that flight, and from a subsequent tour of Australia and New Zealand giving joy-rides. Her first attempt, in the Gipsy Moth G-AALG, (formerly belonging to the Prince of Wales), failed with a crash near Karachi. This flight was between April 9th and 16th 1933, starting from Lympne.

Her second attempt, also from Lympne, started on April 22nd 1934, in a different Moth, G-AARB. Her first backer had withdrawn after the unsuccessful flight, and that Gipsy Moth had been sold. Now she had the backing of that fairy-godfather of aviation, Lord Wakefield. This time the trip ended with damage to the Moth on a forced landing near Rome; but the aircraft was able to be flown back home for repairs and another start. Her best hope, as this was a fifth-hand Moth, and somewhat out-of-date, was to establish a new women's record to Australia. She left on May 8th, beating Amy's record by four days (and Bert Hinkler's time by a few hours) when she reached Darwin on May 23rd. She made her way on to Sydney, over which she was greeted by a fleet of aircraft, including *Southern Cross* (in which she had had her first flight). Later, at Archerfield, Brisbane, she was greeted by 25,000 people. She then shipped G-AARB back home to New Zealand. ▶

95

95. Jean Batten's fifth-hand Gipsy Moth, in which she made her first flight to Australia — and her first flight back, making her the first woman to achieve the two-way flight, in 1935.

96. Jean with her Moth on the way out to Australia, photographed at Calcutta, where engine work had to be done after the discovery of an oil leak which left less than two pints of oil in the sump when she landed.

96

97

97. Jean with her Gull Six, G-ADPR, at Hatfield Aerodrome, probably in 1936 before she set off from there in April on a holiday tour of the Mediterranean with her mother. She had named the Gull Jean, *and it may be indicative of her essentially inward-looking nature, despite her apparently outgoing personality, that she of all the famous fliers of the 1920s and '30s named her aircraft after herself.*

Jean returned to Australia to be there for the finish of the 'MacRobertson' race, and saw Scott and Black flash past the winning line at Melbourne in their Comet, G-ACSS. She was also there, having flown her Moth to Brisbane, when the Duke of Gloucester saw off the mail for England on the first regular air mail service. She now decided to fly back to England for the Jubilee of King George V in May 1935. Still in G-AARB, she left Darwin on April 12th, arriving at Croydon on April 29th. She had taken nearly three days longer than she took on the outward journey.

In 1935 Jean replaced her now ancient Gipsy Moth with a 200hp Percival Gull Six, G-ADPR, which she named *Jean*. She then flew it to South America, starting on November 11th. She had beaten Jim Mollison's record by twenty-four hours, and was the first woman to fly the South Atlantic.

It was in October 1936, at 4.10a.m. on the 5th, that Jean set out to fly *Jean* to Australia in an attempt on the record now held by H.F. (Jim) Broadbent. On November 2nd 1935, Broadbent and C. James (Jimmy) Melrose, both Australians, had each set off at 7 a.m. from Croydon in separate aircraft in individual attempts on the record; Melrose in a Gull Four, VH-UVH, and Broadbent in a Gull Six, VH-UVA. Melrose abandoned his attempt at Singapore to search for Kingsford-Smith, missing in *Lady Southern Cross*, but Broadbent flew on to Darwin, arriving on November 9th after six days, twenty-one hours, nineteen minutes; a new record by seven hours.

Jean Batten made Darwin on October 11th, after five days, twenty-one hours, three minutes — over twenty-four hours under Broadbent's time. She went on to fly home to New Zealand in a new record time from Australia, also setting a new solo record by reaching New Zealand from England in eleven days, one hour, twenty-five minutes. At Auckland, where she landed, she was glad to see her father waiting among the reception party; and the ground was 'black with people'. In early 1937 she returned to Australia, shipping the Gull over at the same time. At Sydney she met Broadbent, who now, since April, held the record from Darwin to England of six days, eight hours, twenty-five minutes (to Lympne). They joked about her beating his records as soon as he had made them, and she said he could keep this one for at least six months. True to her word, it was October 18th when she flew from Darwin in G-ADPR, reaching Lympne on October 24th and lowering his record by fourteen hours, ten minutes. From there, after only twenty minutes, she went on to Croydon. Her mother, who had never before seen the end of any of her flights, was waiting there, having gone on ahead. The welcome far exceeded, as she said herself 'anything I had ever before experienced. It seemed more like a homecoming than just the final landing of a record flight.' This, the last of her great flights, made her the first person to hold both England–Australia and Australia–England records at the same time.

At the beginning of the Second World War, she was staying, in the reported words of her publisher and friend, Robert Pooley, 'with a well-known count' in neutral Sweden. Because of her international reputation she was allowed by the Germans to fly to Britain over their territory. Strangely, she does not seem ever to have flown as a pilot again.

Her personal life is something of an enigma. Despite her glamorous looks and personality she never married — she allegedly turned down at least five proposals — and (unless this is the implication of 'the well-known Count') she does not appear to have been credited with any close personal relationships other than that with her mother, with whom her ties were very strong. Another friend is reported to have said: 'Jean disliked men. That's not to say she loved women, because she didn't. She was a loner.' After her mother died, in 1966, Jean, who was living with her in Tenerife, became something of a recluse. In February 1982 she disappeared from her apartment in Tenerife, telling no-one where she was going. In February 1987 *The Sunday Times Magazine* announced on its front cover: 'Jean Batten is Missing'. Her nephew and heir was attempting to trace her. In September came the news that Jean had in fact died in November 1982, in Majorca, in another apartment; unrecognised and buried in 'a pauper's grave'. It was a sad ending to the story of a great and popular flier, whose greatest achievements were no less for coming so late in the era of international, pioneering, record-making, and record-breaking flights between the two World Wars. •

98

99

98. Jean Batten's Gull Six, Jean, *at Croydon, almost hidden by those allowed near the dais which was erected for official welcomes. A section of the rest of the crowd, which greeted Jean on October 24th 1937 after her last great flight, Darwin to England in five days, eighteen hours, fifteen minutes, is seen in the foreground.*

99. Jean, surrounded by guarding policemen, carried shoulder-high through the crowd at Croydon after her last record-breaking flight. An out-of-focus Aerodrome Hotel is in the background.

POST CAR

This is to certify that

....

has flown with me and

has supported

BRITISH HOSPITALS

AND

BRITISH AVIATION.

Signed................................

100 101

100&101. Charles William Anderson Scott, who first flew G-ACSS, as Grosvenor House, *to Australia, with Tom Campbell Black as co-pilot, to win the MacRobertson race over 12,300 miles in just under seventy-one hours. He had already flown to Australia in 1931 and 1932. This postcard, from the British Hospitals Air Pageant, 1933, has Scott's signature on the back.*

THE COMET RACER, G-ACSS, AND THE FLIGHT OF CLOUSTON AND RICKETTS, CROYDON-AUSTRALIA-NEW ZEALAND-AUSTRALIA-CROYDON, MARCH 1938

On Saturday March 26th 1938, Flying Officer (later Air Commodore) Arthur E. Clouston, together with Victor Ricketts, air correspondent of the *Daily Express*, arrived back at Croydon from Australia and New Zealand in the last great flight of a great aeroplane, the de Havilland D.H.88 Comet, G-ACSS, at this time named *Australian Anniversary*. (It was the one hundred and fiftieth anniversary of European settlement in Australia, as 1988 is the Bicentennial of the same event.) It was also the conclusion of almost the last great flight of the twenty years of pioneering international flight and record-breaking which started in 1919 and ended with the Second World War. The ►

102

102. G-ACSS being built at Hatfield in 1933.

very last solo record-breaking flight before September 1939 was made by Jim Broadbent from Darwin to Lympne between April 18th and 25th, beating Jean Batten's record by three hours, fifty-four minutes; victor, at the end, in their see-saw contest.

It had not been the first trip to Australia for G-ACSS, nor was *Australian Anniversary* the first name she had borne. She had been built as *Grosvenor House* for A.O. Edwards, managing director of the Grosvenor House Hotel, to be flown in the air race of the century, the Mildenhall to Melbourne race of October 1934. This became known as the MacRobertson race, because the entrants were competing for the prize of £15,000 offered by Sir Macpherson Robertson, Melbourne chocolate manufacturer, to celebrate the centenary of the State of Victoria in 1934. *Grosvenor House*, which gained the registration G-ACSS on completion, was one of three Comets built for the race. The others were G-ACSP, *Black Magic*, built for the Mollisons, and G-ACSR, for Bernard Rubin, to be flown by Owen Cathcart-Jones and Ken Waller. *Grosvenor House* was to be flown by C.W.A. Scott and Tom Campbell Black. The D.H.88 was the result of a determination by de Havilland's that the winner of the race should be British. After Sir Macpherson's announcement in March 1933, they offered to design and build a new 200m.p.h. racing aircraft, at a nominal price of £5,000 each, for anyone who would order by February 1934. Three orders were placed. The first Comet to be completed, which became the Mollison's G-ACSP, first flew at Hatfield, piloted by H.S. Broad, on September 8th, only six weeks before the race.

103

103&104. G-ACSS as Australian Anniversary *at Croydon after the Clouston and Ricketts multi-record-breaking flight in March 1938. In the lower picture, the Aerodrome Hotel is seen on the right with crowds watching from the roof.*

As told on p54, *Grosvenor House* was the winner in just under seventy-one hours. The un-named G-ACSR was placed third in the speed class. Second was a Boeing 247 flown by Roscoe Turner and Clyde Pangbourne. Had not Jim and Amy had to drop out at Allahabad with engines damaged by the wrong fuel, the three Comets might have ►

104

105

105. Arthur Clouston (left) and Victor Ricketts (right) greeted by their wives on their return to Croydon in March 1938.

taken all the first three places in the outright speed class (there was also a handicap prize). The race started at dawn on October 20th 1934 from Mildenhall, Suffolk. There were twenty starters, of which nine reached Melbourne within the time limit of sixteen days.

In 1935 G-ACSS was transferred to the R.A.F. for trials as K5084. After a crash-landing she was put up for sale as scrap. She was bought by F.E. Tasker, architect and flier, after Flying Officer Clouston had inspected her, paid a £5 deposit, and persuaded Tasker to pay the rest of the price of £250 and let Clouston use her for racing and long-distance flying! She was rebuilt, re-engined, re-named *The Orphan*, and flown in the Marseilles-Damascus-Paris air race of 1937, where she came fourth, by A.E. Clouston and George Nelson; and then to twelfth place in the King's Cup Race by Ken Waller. Then, as *The Burberry*, G-ACSS left Croydon on November 14th 1937, flown by Clouston and Mrs. Betty Kirby-Green, a friend of a friend who had just got her pilot's licence and offered to raise money for the flight (a hiring fee had to be paid to Tasker — apart from other expenses) if she could go along on the attempt Clouston was planning to make on the record to the Cape. Fortunately, Clouston's fiancée raised no objection. Among other sources, Betty got sponsorship from Burberry's the tailors; hence the new name. On take-off, both Clouston and Betty Kirby-Green were wearing Burberry flying-suits. They beat the record out, arriving on November 16th, and the overall record for the round trip, when they arrived back at Croydon on 20th November, having left on the 18th. They had, in fact, knocked nearly four days off the two-way flight.

It was just over ten weeks later that the Comet, now with her fourth name (the re-christening having been performed at Croydon with a bottle of champagne by Lady Weigall, wife of former Governor-General of Australia) was ready for another record-breaking attempt, this time on the England-Australia record, sponsored by the Australian Consolidated Press to celebrate Australia's hundred and fiftieth anniversary. Clouston, born in New Zealand, privately determined to include his homeland in the trip. (Tasker wanted to attempt the New Zealand record himself, and would only give permission for the flight ending in Australia.) His companion, Ricketts, who was also a pilot, had a let-down typewriter installed above his dual controls. After an abortive first attempt, a second start on March 15th ended at Blenheim, New Zealand, on 20th March, by way of Darwin and Sydney. Their return journey ended at Croydon on 26th March with a tumultuous welcome, despite fog, after the first direct flight to New Zealand and back, in just under six days flying time (not three as crept into the headline on p78 of *The First, the Fastest and the Famous*) over ten days, twenty-one hours, twenty-two minutes. Eleven records were broken on the way, including England-Sydney, Darwin-Sydney and Australia-New Zealand. Tasker's comments on the ignoring of his conditions for hiring G-ACSS do not seem to be recorded.

Victor Ricketts died in the Second World War, on photographic reconnaissance duty in a D.H. Mosquito. A.E. Clouston died in 1984. G-ACSS, restored as *Grosvenor House*, is now in the Shuttleworth Collection at Old Warden Aerodrome, Bedfordshire. •

106. *The 147 Squadron Dakota, with its Australian crew, comes down to land at Croydon with the 'D' hangar block beyond.*

A WARTIME LINK: AN R.A.F. DAKOTA WITH AN AUSTRALIAN CREW AT CROYDON 1944-45

In the early years of the Second World War, Croydon Airport reverted to its World War I use as a defensive aerodrome for London (see *Croydon Airport and the Battle for Britain, 1939-40*). Later, it reverted to a transport role; and in September 1944, No. 147 Squadron, twice before disbanded, was re-formed at Croydon as part of No. 110 Wing, Transport Command (whose HQ was at Croydon), flying Douglas Dakota 3s and 4s. To this squadron were assigned three officers of the R.A.A.F. to form the crew of one of the Dakotas: Flying Officer Tom Carmody, pilot; Flying Officer Ron Halliday, wireless operator; and Flight Lt. Ron Godfrey, navigator. They operated between Croydon and the continent, their duties including carrying home the wounded, and liberated prisoners of war; ferrying fuel to fighter squadrons; and transporting V.I.P.s: once it was General Eisenhower, later President of the United States, to a victory dinner at SHAEF (Supreme Headquarters Allied Expeditionary Force) at Rheims. The squadron remained at Croydon until September 13th 1946, when it was again disbanded, the functions of 110 Wing (and many of its personnel) having been absorbed into the newly-formed British European Airways, which started operations at Croydon. (We hope to tell the full story of this in our next book in the main 'History of Croydon Airport' series). Flying Officer Tom Carmody's twin brother John came to 147 Squadron a few months after Tom, and both stayed until the end of the war. Tom Carmody's last flight for 147 Squadron was on June 2nd 1945. He now lives in Sydney, and Ron Halliday lives in Melbourne. •

107. *The crew of the Dakota at the Victory Dinner at Rheims on the 10th May 1945, to which they had flown General Eisenhower. In front of them are Eisenhower; Air Chief Marshal Sir Arthur Tedder, later Lord Tedder, Deputy Supreme Commander A.E.F. under General Eisenhower; Air Marshal Sir Roderick Carr, Deputy Chief of Staff (Air); and Sqn.Ldr. W. Worth, R.A.A.F., a liaison officer at SHAEF.*

108

108. The Airport. The painted rocks forming C R O ... can be seen in the foreground, in front of the windsock.

CROYDON AIRPORT, QUEENSLAND

In the 1880s, William Chalmers Browne, from Croydon, England, was part-owner of a grazing property known as Croydon Downs Station in Queensland. In 1885 he and his partners discovered gold on the property, and in 1886 Croydon was declared a goldfield. Goldminers flooded in to the district and a town grew up. Its boom years were around 1900 when some 4,500 people lived in Croydon. In 1958, when a 'Back to Croydon Week' was held, the population numbered 170. Nevertheless, Croydon has an airport (more properly aerodrome, no doubt, since an airport should have customs facilities; but Airport is what the citizens of Croydon call it).

In September 1928 the Croydon Shire Council 'Resolved to write to the Doctor in charge of the Aeroplane Ambulance asking that Croydon be made a point of call, if necessary, advising that the Council were prepared to make a landing place and would be pleased to receive particulars as to the requirements of such'. The first aeroplane landed on 28th June 1931, on Archer racecourse, the site subsequently being approved as a landing ground. The first Flying Doctor call was on December 18th, 1934.

In 1979 the Shire Clerk of Croydon, Mr. R.S. Hollands, wrote to Mr. Ewart Sanders, later Secretary of the Croydon Airport Society: '... The airport is well maintained. It is used every Tuesday by the Inland Medical Service doctor, who flies his wife and himself and occasionally a few tourists over for a look at Croydon, Karumba, Normanston and Burketown and it is also used by the Royal Flying Doctor Service every second Friday ... Bush Pilots Airways flies in twice a week ... with mail, passengers and freight ... A veterinary surgeon flies in occasionally, also the Transport Department airport inspectors and chartered planes.

It is a very good all weather aerodrome and was the only means of transport of food and people into Croydon in the 1974 flood when the town was isolated for about eleven weeks ... A passenger terminal building was erected in 1976/77 at a cost of $12,388 ... Before any expected plane lands our aboriginal airport worker, garbage man, etc., Mr. Henry Douglas Snr., has to check that there are no wild pigs, cattle, goats or horses on the strip. It is fenced, but they still get in. [In the early days of Croydon Airport, England, when a farm still occupied part of the site, sheep had to be shooed off to make way for landing aircraft.]

At the side of the airport 'Croydon' is designated by painted rocks forming the letters ... No doubt there is little comparison between the Croydon, England and Croydon, Queensland airports, unfortunately for Croydon, Queensland.'

However, one advantage Croydon Airport, Queensland enjoys over Croydon Airport, England, is that it is still an airport. ●

109

109. The Shire Hall, Croydon, Queensland.

110

110. *Australian-registered Avro Anson, VH-BDX, at Croydon in October, 1950.*

111

111. *Percival Proctor 2, G-ALIS, at Croydon in early 1952, before being flown out to Australia, where it became VH-BQR. It is reported to have been seen at Jandakot, Western Australia, in about 1975.*

12,000-Mile Trip In A Single-Engined Aircraft

"Star" Reporter

TWO Australians, Mr David Maclure and Mr Frank Murphy, take off from Croydon Airport today in a 12-years-old single-engined Proctor aircraft on a 12,000 mile flight to Melbourne.

They will take with them a special message from Lord Home, Secretary of State for Commonwealth Relations, to the Governor of Victoria, and a message of greeting from the Lord Mayor of London, Alderman Cuthbert Ackroyd, to the Lord Mayor of Melbourne, Sir Frank Selleck.

Financing the trip themselves, the two fliers plan to distribute news and information about this year Olympic Games at Melbourne at Paris, Cairo, Karachi, Calcutta, Rangoon, Kuala Lumpur and Singapore.

The plane, which has been decorated with the Olympic insignia, has been fitted with additional tanks to give it a maximum range of 700 miles.

When they arrive in Australia, Mr Maclure and Mr Murphy will set up a company to provide a service of crop and fertiliser spraying from the air.

They hope ultimately to establish a fleet of ex-RAF Tiger Moth aircraft to service a large area of Australian food-producing country.

Sir John Lienhop, Agent-General for Victoria, goes to Croydon today to wish the fliers farewell.

113

113. *The aircraft concerned here is believed to be G-ANGB, which went on to the Australian list as VH-GGB in May 1956.*

112

112. *Percival Proctor 3, G-ALCF, at Croydon, which went to Australia to become VH-AHR in June 1949.*

TO AUSTRALIA FROM CROYDON IN THE LATE 1940s AND 50s — BY PROCTOR AND RAPIDE

After the Second World War, a large number of aircraft became surplus (as had happened in 1918 when the Aircraft Disposal Company was formed at Croydon). No similar organisation appeared in 1945; but the aircraft firms at Croydon were busy for a long time converting the smaller R.A.F. machines, especially the transports and trainers, to civil use. At the beginning, vast numbers of surplus trainer Tiger Moths appeared; but other aircraft followed. One was the D.H.89B Dominie, military version of the D.H.89A Dragon Rapide, to which many Dominies were converted, or converted back. Two which were flown out to Australia are shown here.

Another aircraft to be 'demilitarised' in some ▶

114

114. *The last Percival Proctor 3 to be constructed, G-ANGC, at Croydon in 1957 before going to Australia, where it became VH-BXQ. This is believed to be the Proctor concerned in the story of Rosemary Kirby (right).*

numbers in the 40s and 50s was the Percival Proctor, Mks. 1, 2 and 3, a communications and training aircraft. This was a four-seater aircraft, and after the war became a useful aircraft for charter firms, many of which began by equipping with them, including Air Taxis (Croydon) Ltd. Many, too, were sold overseas, and sometimes Commonwealth servicemen acquired them to fly home in (as had happened after World War One). Here, too, are a number of Proctors which went to Australia, together with two newspaper stories concerning Proctors bound there.

Also in this miscellany is an Australian Avro 652A Anson I. ●

Chronicle · 15 OCT '57

GIRL FLIES OUT TO SEEK JOB AS PILOT

NEWS CHRONICLE REPORTER

OFF to Australia today as an emigrant goes Rosemary Kirby, 29-year-old "odd job girl." But she's no ordinary emigrant. She travels as co-pilot of a 14-year-old, 130 m.p.h. plane.

Rosemary has worked as hotel receptionist, secretary and nursemaid to finance her love of flying.

In six weeks she hopes to have, in Australia, the job she has always wanted—commercial pilot.

The others

At Croydon airfield last night she told me: "I couldn't live without flying.

"Last week-end, after five years, I got my commercial pilot's licence. Now for Australia.

"I've about 300 flying hours to my credit. This trip will add another hundred."

Then Miss Kirby, a bank manager's daughter, of Gloucester Place, St. John's Wood, London, flew off for a couple of hours practice before the big day.

One of her companions on the 9,000-mile trip to Sydney will be 29-year-old dental-surgeon Maurice Thompson, of Sydney, who owns the £800 plane.

Third member of the crew is Australian pharmacist Colin Kennedy, aged 23. He hopes to travel right round the world back to London.

116

116. *De Havilland D.H.89A Dragon Rapide, VH-AIK, registered in 1947 as G-AIWG, received the Australian registration before being flown to Australia in February 1950. Seen here at Croydon before its final departure, this Rapide is reported to have been destroyed by fire at Turkey Creek, Western Australia, on the 29th of September, 1951.*

117. *De Havilland D.H.89A, Dragon Rapide, G-AGSI, (belonging to Olley Air Service) at Croydon in a Control Tower view, before going to Australia to become VH-BFS in October 1954. Beyond is the prototype Miles Gemini G-AGUS, and F-BFVM, another Rapide.*

117

AIR SHOW FOR AMY'S FIFTIETH ANNIVERSARY, CROYDON AIRPORT SITE, MAY 1980

Croydon Airport, after the Second World War, had ceased to be London's chief airport. The R.A.F. departed in 1946, but the new post-war generation of jet airliners needed more space than Croydon could supply. In 1953 the government announced its intention to close Croydon, although there was still considerable activity there with smaller airlines, charter companies, flying-clubs and aircraft engineering, servicing and repairing firms. Despite much opposition, the airport was closed on 30th September 1959. Subsequently, building has taken place on parts of the airport site, including the Roundshaw and Apeldoorn estates, and an industrial estate around the old terminal building and control tower (at present used for office and warehouse space).

Considerable open space, however, remains; and on Bank Holiday Monday May 5th 1980, the 50th anniversary of Amy Johnson's departure for Australia in 1930, the site was opened for flying again for one day, when an air show was held. This had its beginning in a wish by the Council of the London Borough of Sutton to celebrate the occasion.

118

Some of the people, and some of the aircraft, at the Croydon Airport Show, May 1980, seen from the official and press enclosure.

(The whole of the early airport — before 1928 — lay within the present boundaries of Sutton, as did eighty-six per cent of the new, enlarged airport from 1928 onwards). Early suggestions were for the unveiling of commemorative plaques on the Croydon Airport site and in Darwin, the launch of an annual Amy Johnson Memorial Lecture, and a flypast of historic aircraft. This led on, through contacts between the Croydon Airport Society (founded two years earlier) and the Tiger Club of Great Britain, to the offer by the Tiger Club, who fly and promote interest in de Havilland Tiger Moths and other vintage light aircraft, to stage a flying display as part of an air show. This was put to the Council in January 1980 and agreed, and the final show was organised and promoted by what was then Sutton Libraries and Arts Services. It is believed that this is the first time ever that an air show has been arranged and run by a library service. As the organisation of the show progressed, we were fortunate enough to make contact with Amy Johnson's surviving sister, Mrs. Molly Jones, and with Mr. Ron Souch, who was restoring to flying condition a D.H.60G Gipsy Moth, similar to the one Amy had flown to Australia. The re-enactment of Amy's departure became a highlight of the show. ►

119

The buildings of Roundshaw are seen to the right. This housing estate stands roughly on the site of the first airport buildings, 1915-1928. Prominent in the right foreground is a Percival Mew Gull, G-AEXF, and, behind it, a D.H. Puss Moth, G-ABLS.

120

120. The air show was opened by the Australian High Commissioner, Sir James Plimsoll, seen here being driven round the field before the opening of the show in a vintage Bentley car. Left to right: owner of the car; Sue Thompson, pilot, who was to represent Amy Johnson; Mrs. Molly Jones, née Johnson; Sir James Plimsoll.

The production and issuing of a special commemorative philatelic 'flown cover' by Sutton in co-operation with the R.A.F. Museum at Hendon and the Croydon Airport Society was another; and the launching of the second volume in Sutton Libraries' 'History of Croydon Airport' series: *Croydon Airport: The Great Days, 1928-1939* was arranged to coincide.

A very great deal of work was accomplished in a very short time by the staff of Sutton Libraries, and other Council departments as well; and May 5th dawned — chilly, windy, cloudy, but basically fine. The crowds who came exceeded even the optimistic hopes of the organisers, and were estimated at some 50,000.

Purley Way was jammed as it had not been jammed since the famous flights of the 1930s finished at Croydon — or since Amy herself returned there on that day in August 1930. On the ground there were sideshows, trade stands with goods ranging through motor cars, model aircraft and tee-shirts; arts and crafts stalls including specially designed jewellery and artefacts commemorating Amy's flight; and refreshments of many kinds. Before the main flying started, there was the arrival of the Tiger Club aircraft and others to be seen; and arena events which included music, gymnastics, karate, and radio-controlled and control-line model aircraft flying. The Tiger club did close-formation flying, aerobatic displays, ribbon-cutting near the ground, flour-bombing and wing-walking. There was a parachuting display. In the middle of the show the re-enactment of Amy's flight took place in Ron Souch's Gipsy Moth, G-ABEV named *Joan*, after his wife, and painted bottle-green like Amy's *Jason*. It was flown by Sue Thompson, dressed as Amy had been dressed, in a flying-suit matching the colour of her aircraft. She flew to Gatwick, taking with her a plaque, letters, and flown covers, for onward transmission to Darwin by Qantas. Many press and TV cameras were present; but this was the day of the storming by the S.A.S. of the Iranian Embassy to release hostages being held there, and that cornered all television news coverage that evening.

Still, it had been a 'Great Day' at Croydon Airport, and a handsome profit was made to justify Sutton Council's enterprise ... and now we are doing it again.

This book is being published to coincide with another Tiger Club air show on the Croydon Airport site, on May 30th 1988. This time we are celebrating several things: the Australian Bicentennial; the 60th anniversary of the opening of the enlarged Croydon Airport and its new buildings on May 2nd, 1928 by Lady Maud Hoare, wife of Sir Samuel Hoare, Secretary of State for Air; the flight of Bert Hinkler from Croydon into undying fame on February 7th 1928, sixty years ago; and the memory of all those others who flew to or from Australia, leaving Croydon or arriving there, seen off by a handful of people or welcomed back by tens of thousands; and the many Croydon characters concerned with the forging of air links across two hemispheres. These links now begin and end at places other than Croydon, but Croydon's part in their making will never be forgotten. In token of this it is hoped that within the next few years a museum of Croydon Airport, and of civil aviation in general, will be established in part of the airport terminal building (now Airport House) through the Croydon Airport Society by the courtesy of the building's present owners, the Guardian Royal Exchange Assurance plc, who have announced this as their intention. •

121

121. Sir James Plimsoll speaking in the Aerodrome Hotel before the unveiling of one of the two plaques commemorating Amy's flight. Both plaques (the other is now in Darwin) were donated by the Croydon Airport Society. On the left is Councillor Edward Trevor, then Mayor of the London Borough of Sutton. Croydon Airport: The Great Days *was launched at the same ceremony.*

LONDON BOROUGH OF SUTTON

The Worshipful the Mayor
Councillor Edward G Trevor FRICS

Mayor's Parlour, Civic Offices, St Nicholas Way, Sutton, Surrey SM1 1EA
tel: 01 - 661 5058

The Worshipful the Mayor of Darwin
Alderman Dr Ella Stack
Town Hall
Darwin
Australia

5th May 1980

Dear Mr Mayor,

Fifty years ago today a 26 year old English girl set off from Croydon Airport on a flight which was to catch the public's imagination and ensure that Amy Johnson's name would go into the history books.

We, in the London Borough of Sutton are delighted to have this opportunity to mark her daring flight by re-opening Croydon Airport for the day - in itself an historic event.

I would like to extend to you, Mr Mayor, and all the citizens of Darwin warmest greetings together with my sincere hope that the links of friendship which Amy's flight established, and which have continued between our countries throughout the past fifty years, will remain and strengthen over at least the next fifty years.

You may be interested to know that our Coat of Arms has the rising sun at the foot of the shield with an Hannibal aircraft representing Croydon Airport. This is the first coat of arms in the world to show an aircraft and in 1965 when the London Borough of Sutton was formed it was our special wish to retain our links with the historic site by including this symbol in our town's Coat of Arms.

The 5th May is an historic day for the aviation world and all the many famous names gathered here today join me in sending our combined salute to a brave lady.

Yours sincerely

Edward G Trevor

Mayor.

122

122. Letter from the Mayor of Sutton to the Mayor of Darwin sent in the mail which started on its way to Darwin from Croydon in the Gipsy Moth flown to Gatwick by Sue Thompson. Another letter which travelled the same way to the Mayor of Darwin was from Sir Peter Masefield, President of the Croydon Airport Society.

123

123. The plaque commemorating her sister's historic flight, after unveiling by Mrs. Molly Jones in the Aerodrome Hotel.

124

124. Molly Jones and Sue Thompson hold between them the second plaque, which is now in the Civic Centre at Port Darwin, where it was unveiled on 17th July 1980 by Miss Jan Schonburg, who followed Amy's route out to Australia flying solo in a Cessna 150 and arrived in Darwin on that day. She had left on May 5th from Denham, and had flown over Croydon in the morning to dip her wings in salute before heading for the coast. Sue Thompson was about to fly the Gipsy Moth G-ABEV to Gatwick. From there, the helicopter link took plaque, flown covers and official letters across to Heathrow, from where Qantas flew them out to Darwin. The covers stamped and signed to authenticate their journey, were then flown back to England by Qantas for sale.

125. *One of the philatelic flown covers which went to Darwin and back. The signatures at the top are of Molly Jones and Sue Thompson.*

126. Advertisement, c. *1930, showing some of those who had flown to Australia by then.*

SELECT BIBLIOGRAPHY

The following books have been invaluable throughout for the information they contain:

Davies, R.E.G. — A History of the World's Airlines. O.U.P. 1964, 1967
Jackson, A.J. — British Civil Aircraft since 1919. 2nd ed. 3 vols. Putnam, 1973
Lewis, Peter — British Racing and Record-Breaking Aircraft. Putnam, 1971
Stroud, John — Annals of British and Commonwealth Air Transport 1919–1960. Putnam, 1962
Wixted, Edward P. — The North-West Aerial Frontier, 1919–1934. Boolarong Publications, Brisbane, 1985

Also invaluable, and recommended for further reading on individual fliers, are:
Barker, Ralph — Verdict on a Lost Flyer: The Story of Bill Lancaster. Harrap, 1969
Batten, Jean — My Life. Harrap, 1938. (Paperback ed. published as Alone in the Sky. Airlife Publishing, 1979)
Chichester, Francis — The Lonely Sea and the Sky. Hodder and Stoughton, 1964
Clouston, A.E. — The Dangerous Skies. Cassell, 1954
Davis, Pedr — Charles Kingsford Smith: The World's Greatest Aviator. Lansdowne Press, Sydney, 1985
Davis, Pedr & Smith, Dick — Kookaburra: The Most Compelling Story in Australia's Aviation History. Lansdowne Press, Sydney, 1980
MacKenzie, R.D. — Solo: The Bert Hinkler Story. Jacaranda Press, Brisbane/Angus and Robertson, London
McNally, Ward — Smithy. Hale, 1966
Mollison, James — Playboy of the Air. Michael Joseph, 1937
Smith, Constance Babington — Amy Johnson. Collins, 1967

and, of course, our Croydon Airport publications (see below)

HISTORY OF CROYDON AIRPORT BOOKS

The 'History of Croydon Airport' books, published by Sutton Leisure, are mentioned in various places in this book. They are, so far:

1. *The First Croydon Airport, 1915–1928*
   by Bob Learmonth, Joanna Nash, Douglas Cluett (editor). 1977.
2. *Croydon Airport: The Great Days, 1928–1939*
   by Douglas Cluett, Joanna Nash and Bob Learmonth. 1980.
3. *Croydon Airport and the Battle for Britain, 1939–40*
   by Douglas Cluett, Joanna Bogle (Nash) and Bob Learmonth. 1984.

The First, The Fastest and the Famous: a Cavalcade of Croydon Airport Events and Celebrities by Douglas Cluett. 1985.

Also published by Sutton Leisure:
Croydon Airport Flypast: Historic Aircraft Profiles in Colour. Written and illustrated by Peter G. Cooksley. 1984.
Croydon Airport Remembered: An Aviation Artist Looks Back, Written and illustrated by Charles Couper Dickson. 1985.
Croissants at Croydon: the Memoirs of Jack Bamford (General Manager in Great Britain of Air Union, later Air France, from 1930 to 1965). Published in association with Les Anciens d'Air France, 1986.